D0596973

THE 10 THINGS YOU NEED TO KNOW ABOUT ISLAM

RON RHODES

HARVEST HOUSE PUBLISHERS

EUGENE, OREGON

Cover photo © Sylvester Adams / Photodisc Red / Getty Images

Cover by Terry Dugan Design, Minneapolis, Minnesota

THE 10 THINGS YOU NEED TO KNOW ABOUT ISLAM
Copyright © 2007 by Ron Rhodes
Published by Harvest House Publishers
Eugene, Oregon 97402

ISBN: 978-0-7394-8669-6

Printed in the United States of America

To Christians everywhere who seek
to share the good news of Jesus with
Muslim friends and neighbors.

ACKNOWLEDGMENTS

Every once in a while, when everyone in our family is in the same room, someone will call out, "Group hug!" That's our cue to drop whatever we're doing and enjoy a quick family hug together.

Upon completion of this book, I called for a group hug with my wife, Kerri, and our two children, David and Kylie, to express heartfelt thanks to them for their incredible love and support during the writing of this book. I am eternally grateful to God for our wonderful family.

CONTENTS

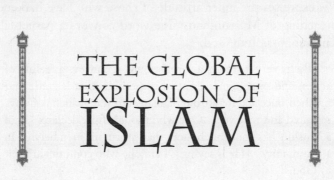

THE GLOBAL EXPLOSION OF ISLAM

THIS BOOK IS INTENTIONALLY CONCISE. There is something to be said for brevity. However, brevity should not be confused with superficiality.

In an age of information overload, this book is intended to provide you with the most relevant and helpful information on Islam in the briefest possible fashion. In the short time it takes you to read this book, you will become well-versed in the Muslim worldview, Muslim theology, Muslim ethics, and the Muslim view of Christianity. Consider this book to be a crash course on the controversial world of Islam.

The Birth of Islam

Islam is a monotheistic religion that arose in the seventh century AD under the leadership of Muhammad (also spelled *Muhammed* and *Mohammed*). Muhammad was allegedly the greatest of a long line of prophets that included Moses and Jesus. His primary revelation was that the one true God is Allah. Allah's revelation to Muhammad occurred over a 23-year period and is recorded in the Quran (Islam's holy book, also spelled *Koran*). *Quran* means "that which is to be read."

Islam literally means "submission to the will of Allah." Members of Islam are called *Muslims* ("those who submit"). The word *Muslim* expresses the inner attitude of those who have harkened to the preaching of Muhammad.[1] The word conveys a perpetual and ongoing submission to God.

> By its very form [as a verbal noun] it conveys a feeling of action and ongoingness, not of something that is static and finished, once and for all, but of an inward state which is always repeated and renewed...One who thoughtfully declares "I am a Muslim" has done much more than affirm his membership in a community...[He is saying] "I am one who commits himself to God."[2]

Islam involves beliefs (the five doctrines of Islam) and obligations (the five pillars of Islam), which I will discuss in greater detail throughout the book.

The Mosque: The Muslim Place of Worship

The word *mosque* comes from the word *masjid,* which literally means "a place of prostration or prayer." The Muslim mosque is considered a place of worship, prayer, and fellowship. Muslims believe that prayer in a mosque is far more effective than prayer anywhere else (Hadith 1:620).

Muslim mosques come in a variety of shapes and sizes. They typically have a prayer room with rugs for sitting and kneeling during prayer rituals. A niche in the wall indicates the direction of Mecca (a Saudi Arabian capital toward which worshippers offer prayers). Muslim leaders deliver sermons from an elevated platform. Larger mosques may include a library with Islamic literature, a social hall for fellowship, rooms dedicated to Quranic study, and living quarters for resident leaders. Some mosques contain a school for training the *mullahs* (or *ulama*—Islamic scholars).[3]

Muslims have no ordained clergy. Generally, Muslim leaders emerge because of their personal knowledge of the Quran and their oratory skills.

Women are prohibited from entering a mosque during their menstrual period. One scholar notes, "Younger women are strongly discouraged from entering the mosque because they might carelessly enter in a state of impurity. Hindered from praying in the mosque, women have a harder time having their sins forgiven."[4]

The Growth of Islam

About 20 percent of the earth's population is Muslim. That's about 1.3 billion people—one out of every five persons on earth!

The Muslim world was once "somewhere else." No longer. Islam is now part and parcel of life in the United States. George Braswell comments, "Christians are discovering that they have Muslim neighbors, that mosques are being built next to churches, that their medical doctors are Muslims, and that their children attend school with Muslims."[5]

The United States presently has more than 3000 Muslim mosques; in 1990 there were only 30.[6] A new mosque opens each week in the United States. As of this writing, 165 Islamic schools, 426 Islamic associations, and 90 Islamic publications are located in the United States.[7] An Islamic leader inaugurated a session of the United States Senate, praying in the name of Allah.[8]

Some well-known Muslims live in this country. Among these are pop musician Cat Stevens, who converted to Islam in 1977 and changed his name to Yusuf Islam. He and basketball stars Kareem Abdul-Jabbar and Hakeem Olajuwon have generated substantial publicity for the religion.

Islam has enjoyed impressive growth around the world:

- Islam is presently the world's second-largest religion. (Christianity is the largest.)
- More than 65 nations in the world are Islamic.
- Muslims constitute about 85 percent of the population in 32 countries.[9]
- Islam is now the second-largest religion in Europe.[10]

- Muslims outnumber Methodists and Baptists combined in the United Kingdom.[11]
- England had only one mosque in 1945, but now it has thousands. Hundreds of the buildings currently used for mosques were originally churches—including the church that sent well-known Christian missionary William Carey to India.[12]
- India alone has more than 100 million Muslims.[13]
- Muslims comprise the second-largest religious group in France. The number of mosques in France mushroomed from only one in 1974 to thousands today.[14]
- Muslims constitute a majority in 45 African and Asian countries.[15]
- China has 100 million Muslims.[16]
- Indonesia has more than 180 million Muslims.[17]
- Saudi Arabia and other Muslim countries are currently donating tens of millions of dollars to promote Islam in the United States.[18]

Many Muslims argue that the explosive growth of Islam around the world constitutes proof that Islam is *the* true religion. After all, how could the religion grow so exponentially without God's blessing?[19]

Reasons for Islamic Growth

Islam is growing around the world for several reasons. Here are some of the most pertinent factors that Muslim leaders acknowledge:

Financial support. A great deal of money is being poured into Arab missions around the world, especially in the United States. This money is being used to build mosques, create Islamic centers at major universities, and publish Islamic literature.[20]

A universal religion. Islam claims to be a universal religion. Though it originated in Mecca, it claims to be for all people everywhere. Islam claims to know no barriers between races.[21] (Interestingly, though, the

Shi'ites, Sunnis, and other Muslim sects disagree on key issues and divide from one another.)

A simple religion. Islam has few requirements. It is a much simpler religion, Muslims claim, than Christianity. It contains no difficult doctrines like the Trinity and the two natures (divine and human) in the one person of Christ. A person who recites the Islamic creed is a Muslim. A person who keeps the five pillars (ethical principles) of Islam is a *good* Muslim. A person who emulates the life of Muhammad (as recorded in Islamic tradition—the Hadith) will be a *successful* Muslim.

A comprehensive religion. Muslims say that Islam, unlike Christianity, encompasses all of life—political, economic, judicial, social, moral, and religious. (Christians believe a relationship with Christ affects one's interactions in all these realms.)

An easier-to-obey religion. Muslims say Islam is a much easier religion to obey than Christianity. Many of Christ's teachings seem almost impossible to fulfill (for example, His requirements in the Sermon on the Mount). In contrast, the Quran's commands are realistic, and the average person can obey them. (Christians believe that though Christ's commands are indeed loftier, the indwelling Holy Spirit empowers people to successfully live the Christian life.)

A rational religion. Certain doctrines in Christianity do not make sense to Muslims. For example, the idea that one man can die for another or for many people, or the idea that God cannot forgive people without sacrificing someone on a cross, is nonsensical to them. In contrast, Islam is a thinking man's religion. It contains no irrational concepts as does Christianity. (I will address these issues later in the book.)

A brotherhood religion. Muslims all over the world follow the Muslim Hadith (traditions), which contain details on how Muhammad acted in various circumstances, so they have a sense of camaraderie and brotherhood few other religious groups experience.

Proselytizing. Muslims proselytize. They actively share their faith. They are commanded in the Quran to "invite (all) to the way of thy Lord with wisdom" (Sura 16:125).[22]

Colliding Faiths: Islam Versus Christianity

The denials Islam makes regarding Christianity relate not to peripheral issues over which people can feel free to disagree in an agreeable way. Rather, Islam's denials cut to the very heart of Christianity. Islam claims that the Christian Bible has been corrupted, that God is not a Trinity, that Jesus is not God or the Son of God or even the Savior, that Jesus did not die on the cross for the sins of humanity, and that Jesus did not rise from the dead. In other words, Islam denies what Christianity regards as nonnegotiable.[23]

The debate between Christianity and Islam is a critically important one.

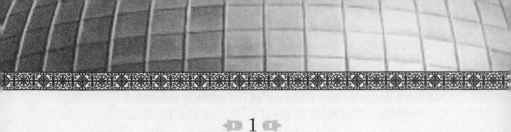

UNITY AND
DIVERSITY AMONG
MUSLIMS

MUSLIMS DO NOT ALL BELIEVE THE SAME THINGS.
Though Muslims often criticize Christianity for having so many different denominations and divisions within it, many sects and divisions exist within Islam, some estimates placing the figure around 150.[1] World religions scholar Lewis Hopfe is correct in his assessment that Islam is not a monolithic body. "Although most Muslims would agree on the basic principles of Islam, there are many variations in beliefs and practices."[2] In short, we see both unity and diversity in the Muslim world.

Unity: The Five Essential Beliefs

Muslims subscribe to five essential doctrines. Belief in these five essentials is common to Muslims everywhere:

God. The one true God's name is Allah. The term *Allah* is probably derived from *al illah,* which means "the god." Allah has seven primary characteristics. He has absolute unity—that is, he is one and not a Trinity (God cannot have a son or a partner). He is also all-seeing, all-hearing, all-speaking, all-knowing, all-willing, and all-powerful.

Angels. A hierarchy of angels stretches between Allah and humankind. The chief is Gabriel, the archangel who gave revelations to Muhammad (Sura 2:97). Each human being has two recording angels who list all of his or her deeds, good or bad (Sura 50:17). These recorded deeds will be reviewed at the coming judgment.

Holy books. The four inspired books are the Torah of Moses, the Psalms of David, the Gospel of Jesus Christ, and the Quran (containing the teachings of Muhammad). The Quran contains Allah's final message to humankind and supersedes all previous revelations. The Quran abrogates any conflicting truth claims. Only the Quran has been preserved to the present time in an uncorrupted state.

Prophets. Throughout history, 124,000 prophets have been sent to humanity. The most important ones number less than 30—the greatest of whom is Muhammad. Other prominent prophets include Adam, Noah, Abraham, Moses, David, Solomon, Jonah, John the Baptist, and Jesus. Each prophet brought truth for his particular age, but Muhammad is a prophet for all time.

A future judgment. A future resurrection and day of judgment will both occur. Allah will be the judge. Allah weighs people's good and bad deeds and sends people to paradise (a place of pleasure) or to hell (a place of torment).

Fate. Some Muslims teach a sixth doctrine—that Allah foreordains all things. He is totally sovereign. Nothing can take place without Allah ordaining it to happen. No event is random.

I will address these doctrines in greater detail throughout the rest of this book.

Diversity Among Muslims

Muslim clerics may well teach different things in different parts of the world. For example, in the United States, Muslim clerics often say that Islam is a religion of peace and does not sanction terrorism. In Saudi Arabia, Iran, and other such countries, however, Muslim clerics predominantly teach that unbelievers (including Jews and Christians) must be fought until they are subdued.[3] This latter group of clerics divides people into two categories: those who submit to the will of Allah and those who do not.

This diversity of views among Muslim clerics is not surprising. Different parts of the Quran communicate seemingly contradictory messages regarding how to treat unbelievers. As researcher David Goldman puts it, "Some revelations in the Quran are kind to non-Muslims. Other revelations are adversarial. Either position can be argued by quoting specific Quranic verses."[4]

To make matters worse for United States citizens, many Muslims are angry at the United States because of its relationship with Israel. Many Arab Muslims believe Israel is essentially an outpost for American expansionism. Militant Muslims have made no secret about their desire to return Israeli territory to Muslim control. They promise there will not be peace until they obtain that control.

The Sunnis

Islam has two majors sects—the Sunnis and the Shi'ites. These sects originally divided over a dispute about the first *caliph* (successor) to Muhammad, whom Muhammad neglected to appoint prior to his death. The Sunnis said Muhammad's successor should be elected. The Shi'ites believed the successor should come through Muhammad's bloodline. The Sunnis got their way. They accept the first four caliphs—Abu Bakr, Omar, Othman, and Ali—as the legitimate successors to Muhammad.

The Sunnis make up about 90 percent of all Muslims and predominate in Egypt, Saudi Arabia, and Pakistan. Their name is derived from *Sunnah*, which refers to "the trodden path" or "tradition." The Sunnis are the traditionalists of Islam.

Toward this end, Sunnis everywhere seek to live their lives according to the exemplary pattern set by Muhammad (as recorded in Muslim tradition) and to obey the Quran. Sunnis believe their Muslim faith can be lived out in the context of various existing earthly governments.[5] Sunnis are generally more tolerant of diversity than are Shi'ites, so Sunnis adapt more easily to divergent cultures around the world.

The Shi'ites

Shi'ites constitute only about 10 percent of the Muslim world, but they are nevertheless the most visible and vocal of all the Muslim sects. The term *Shi'ite* is a corruption of the term *Shi'at Ali,* which means "partisans of Ali," and refers to the fact that they have rejected all subsequent caliphs who were not descendants of Ali (Muhammad's son-in-law).[6] The Shi'ites predominate in Iran, Iraq, Lebanon, and parts of Africa. They are much more literal than Sunnis in their interpretation and application of the Quran, and they are much more militant. The Shi'ites view government as a divine institution of Allah, and they attempt to establish a theocracy (God-ruled nation) on earth.[7]

Shi'ites tend to view the present world order with great distrust. They admire true believers in Allah, those who tenaciously cling to their faith and refuse to sell out to the established order.[8] Shi'ites do not compromise with unbelievers.

Shi'ite leaders are known by the title *Imam,* and they wield extreme authority over their subjects. They are fiercely authoritarian in their interpretation of the Quran and believe that Allah speaks through them. World religions specialist Dean Halverson says the Imam is the Muslim counterpart to the Catholic pope.[9] Shi'ites believe a divine spark and the "light of Muhammad" are passed from one Imam to the next.[10] Ayatollah Khomeini, who died in 1989, was an Imam.[11]

Differing Views on the Jihad

Muhammad never mentioned jihad early in his career. This was certainly the case when he was living initially in Mecca. Scholars have suggested that the reason for this is that during those early years he lacked a strong following and military might. Once in Medina, however, he was able to build a strong following and a strong military. Jihad suddenly became a topic of major Quranic revelation.[12] Note the following contrasts in Muhammad's behavior in Mecca and Medina:

	MECCA	MEDINA
evangelism	by preaching	by the sword
personal behavior	priestlike	warriorlike

marriage	one wife, Khadija	eleven more wives in ten years
focus of battle	against idol worship	against Jews and Christians
nature of Islam	religious movement	political movement[13]

Jihad comes from the Arabic word *jahada,* which principally means "to struggle" or "to strive in the path of Allah." The term has made headlines many times in recent years, especially in connection with terrorist activities around the world. Muslims generally understand it to refer to armed fighting and warfare in defending Islam and standing against evil.

Some Muslims, however, have held to less dangerous forms of jihad. One example of this is a jihad *of the pen*—a written defense of Islam.[14]

In keeping with this, scholar Frederick Mathewson Denny notes that "holy war" doesn't fully capture the meaning of jihad, although that is certainly part of it. Denny says that Muslims refer to a greater jihad and a lesser jihad. A person's struggle with his own vices, the evil tendencies in his soul, and his lack of faith is considered the greater jihad. This jihad is a spiritual struggle or striving. Many Muslims in the United States hold to this interpretation of jihad.

Engaging in armed struggle against the enemies of Islam is considered the lesser jihad.[15] Islam scholar Jamal Elias claims that for most Muslims today, "any war that is viewed as a defense of one's own country, home, or community is called a jihad. This understanding is very similar to what is called 'just war' in Western society."[16]

Radical Islamic fundamentalists are well-known for their use of arms and explosives in defending their version of Islam. Jihad, in their thinking, can terrorize perceived enemies of Islam into submission and retreat.[17]

Such Muslims emulate the behavior of Muhammad (Sura 33:21), for he often led Islamic forces into battle to make Islam dominant during his time. He shed other people's blood to bolster Islam throughout the Arabian Peninsula.[18] In fact, "Muhammad's mission was to conquer the world for Allah. The goal of jihad, or holy war, is to establish Islamic authority over the whole world. Islam teaches that Allah is the only authority, and all political systems must be based on Allah's teaching."[19] Islamic history clearly reveals that jihad has been a primary tool of Islamic expansion.

This radical form of jihad is taken much more seriously today than it used to be because of the sheer number of radical Muslims threatening various countries and because of the growing availability of weapons of mass destruction. Though radical Islamic fundamentalists constitute a relative minority of Muslims, even a minority can be a substantial threat. John Ankerberg and John Weldon explain that "since we are talking about 1.3 billion adherents to Islam, even a 'very small minority' can involve tens of millions of people who have the potential to cause a great deal of trouble in the world, not only for America, but for moderate Muslim governments as well."[10]

Islamic fundamentalists often cite verses from the Quran to support their view that arms are permissible and even compulsory in the defense of Islam. In Sura 2:216 we read, "Fighting is prescribed for you, and ye dislike it. But it is possible that ye dislike a thing which is good for you." In Sura 47:4 we read, "Therefore, when ye meet the unbelievers (in fight), smite at their necks; At length, when ye have thoroughly subdued them, bind a bond firmly (on them)." Sura 9:5 says, "But when the forbidden months are past, then fight and slay the pagans wherever ye find them, and seize them, beleaguer them, and lie in wait for them in every stratagem (of war)."

In 1998 five Muslim *caliphates* (governments)—representing five radical Muslim factions—signed a *fatwa* (written decision) declaring a holy war against the United States. The document they signed contains the following words:

> For over seven years the United States has been occupying the lands of Islam and the holiest of places, the Arabian Peninsula, plundering its riches, dictating to its rulers, humiliating its people, terrorizing its neighbors, and turning its bases in the Peninsula into a spearhead through which to fight the neighboring

Muslim peoples...[There has been] aggression against the Iraqi people...[Their aim has been to] serve the Jews' petty state... [They express] eagerness to destroy Iraq...All these crimes and sins committed by the Americans are a clear declaration of war on Allah, his messenger, and Muslims...The ruling to kill the Americans and their allies—civilians and military—is an individual duty for every Muslim who can do it in any country in which it is possible to do it...This is in accordance with the words of Almighty Allah, "and fight the pagans altogether as they fight you altogether," and "fight them until there is no more tumult or oppression, and there prevail justice and faith in Allah."[21]

Who can doubt that the September 11, 2001, attack against the World Trade Center and Pentagon was prompted by this fatwa, written just three years earlier? Americans have taken jihad very seriously since that day.

Many Muslims are religiously motivated to participate in jihad, for any Muslim who loses his or her life in service to Allah is guaranteed entrance into paradise (Hadith 9:459). According to Muslim tradition, Muhammad said, "The person who participates in [holy battles] in Allah's cause and nothing compels him to do so except belief in Allah and His Apostles, will be recompensed by Allah either with a reward, or booty [if he survives] or will be admitted to Paradise [if he is killed in the battle as a martyr]" (Hadith 1:35). That is why an Islamic suicide bomber is willing to give up his or her life.

The Call to Evangelism

Despite all this talk about jihad, many Muslims who call the United States their home are peace-loving people who do not endorse terrorist acts. They are excellent prospects for evangelism.

Sadly, more than one Christian missionary has noted that very few people seem to convert from Islam to Christianity. The truth is, Muslim conversions seem few not because Muslims are so hard to convert but because the Christian church has largely ignored them. A mere 2 percent of the Protestant missionary force is actively involved in evangelizing among 1.3 billion Muslims.[22] William Miller says that "with some glorious exceptions, the Christians of the world have signally failed to obey Christ by sending laborers to sow and reap a harvest in Muslim lands."[23] Not only are too few Christian missionaries evangelizing Muslims in other countries, far too few Christians are seeking to reach Muslims in our own country. This is not as it should be.

Jesus, though not speaking specifically about Muslims, nevertheless made a statement very much needed for this hour: "The harvest is plentiful but the workers are few. Ask the Lord of the harvest, therefore, to send out workers into his harvest field" (Matthew 9:37-38). The apostle Paul also spoke eloquent words needed for our times: "How, then, can they call on the one they have not believed in? And how can they believe in the one of whom they have not heard? And how can they hear without someone preaching to them?" (Romans 10:14).

Let's not forget that Christ calls us to be His witnesses to all peoples and all nations (Matthew 24:14; 28:19; Mark 16:15; Luke 24:47)—including Muslims. And let us not be shy about it. We must boldly tell the truth about Jesus to our Muslim acquaintances and pray earnestly that God would work in the hearts of those we speak to. We can praise the Lord that Muslims are coming to know Jesus Christ each and every day.

⬧ 2 ⬧

THE QURAN: THE
SCRIPTURE
OF ISLAM

MUSLIMS' RESPECT FOR THE QURAN cannot be overstated. The Quran is the most revered and venerated book in any Muslim home. It is called "the Mother of books." The first thing Muslims hear upon birth and the last thing they hear just before the moment of death is a reading from the Quran. Muslims often inscribe verses from the Quran on the walls of their homes. The Quran is also a textbook on Islam for Muslim children.

Muslims typically do not touch the Quran without first having washed and purified themselves. They recite the Quran daily. Some Muslims become professional reciters. Such recitation is considered an art form, and high acclaim is given to individuals who do it well, adding inflections so that each verse rings out with a musical quality.[1]

Many Muslims, including children, memorize the Quran. This is considered a great act of piety, and those who do so receive great respect.[2] Pious Muslims seek to read a thirtieth of the Quran each night so they can finish the Quran every month.[3] A daily recitation from the Quran supposedly keeps Satan away from the home.[4]

Muslims often carry the Quran with them into war, believing it will bring them Allah's blessing and protection. Sometimes Muslims suspend copies of the Quran around their necks, much like a charm.[5]

Writing out a copy of the Quran by hand brings merit before Allah. Many great Islamic men of the past, including Islamic leaders, have engaged in this exercise.[6]

Muslims typically view the Quran as a miraculous wonder:

> The Quran is the greatest wonder among the wonders of the world. It repeatedly challenged the people of the world to bring a chapter like it, but they failed and the challenge remains unanswered up to this day...This book is second to none in the world according to the unanimous decision of the learned men in points of diction, style, rhetoric, thoughts and soundness of laws and regulations to shape the destinies of mankind.[7]

In Islamic bookstores, the general practice is to not attach a price tag to copies of the Quran. After all, the Quran is priceless. Instead, the proper etiquette is for a customer to ask the storekeeper what a suitable "gift" would be for the priceless book.[8]

Muslims treat their copies of the Quran with great respect. The book is never to be laid on the ground and is not to come into contact with any unclean substance. Nothing is ever to be placed on top of it. It is often wrapped in a beautiful cover, and is typically read from an ornate stand specially made for holding it.[9] When not in use, it is often placed on a small ledge near the ceiling, thus occupying the highest place in the home.

THE MUSLIM VIEW OF THE QURAN

Finality

Muslims believe Allah's revelation is eternal, so the substance of all the holy books that derive from him are the same. But how are we to account for the differences between, for example, the Quran and the Christian Bible? The most common answer is that copyists tampered with the Bible through the years, so what passes as the Bible today is not the same as the Bible originally given to man. Other Muslims point to a progressive nature to Allah's revelation to humankind, for man was not always ready for the fullness of his message. Man was only given as much as he could digest at the time. These progressively more comprehensive revelations from Allah culminated in the Quran, which is Allah's final and complete revelation to humankind.[10]

Arrangement of the Quran

The Quran contains 114 Suras (chapters), arranged in order according to length, with the longer chapters first and the shorter ones last. This arrangement often confuses non-Muslim readers, who are accustomed to books arranged by topic, genre, or chronology.[11] The Quran contains a total of 6247 verses and is about four-fifths the length of the New Testament.

An Exact Copy of Heaven's Original

Muslims believe the Quran is an exact and faithful reproduction of the original in heaven—an engraved tablet that has existed for all eternity in the presence of Allah.[12] The angel Gabriel took more than 20 years to bring the Quran to Muhammad, communicating only isolated sections at any single time, portion by portion, while Muhammad was in a prophetic trance. The Quran is thus viewed not as the word of Muhammad but as the very word of Allah.

Because Gabriel brought the Quran from heaven to earth in its original Arabic form, the Arabic language is considered an essential component of the Quran. Many Muslims believe the Quran cannot be divorced from the Arabic language. Therefore, unlike Christians, who translate the Bible into as many languages as possible, Muslims have always been reluctant to publish the Quran in other languages for non-Arabic readers.

Compiling the Quran

At Muhammad's death in AD 632, no complete manuscript of the Quran existed. Former Muslims Ergun Mehmet Caner and Emir Fethi Caner note that "Islam teaches that Muhammad did not foresee his death, and made no preparations for the compilation of his revelations. The work of collecting the revelations fell to Muhammad's patriots."[13]

When Muhammad uttered his revelations, his followers generally recorded them on any material that was available—including bits of parchment, leaves, flat stones, and pieces of bone (such as the shoulder blades of camels). Of course, many of his followers also memorized his sayings. All these fragmented recordings of Muhammad's revelations had to be collected, and this process took time.[14] The compilation took place between AD 646 and 650.

About a year after Muhammad's death, at the prompting of Umar (who would later become the second caliph), some of Muhammad's companions ordered the collection of the Quran for fear that it might fade away. Zaid, a trusted secretary of Muhammad, was appointed to the task. Zaid said, "During the lifetime of the prophet the Quran had all been written down, but it was not yet united in one place nor arranged in successive order."[15] So Zaid engaged in collecting bits and pieces of revelation in order to compile this initial version.

Some time later, Uthman, the third caliph, heard that several Muslim communities in Syria, Armenia, and Iraq were reciting the Quran in a way that was different from the way those in Arabia were reciting it. This was unacceptable to Uthman. Islam would be damaged if different versions of the Quran were in wide distribution. Uthman thus called upon Zaid to oversee the production of a definitive and final authorized version of the Quran that would become the standard for all Muslims everywhere.[16] Once Zaid completed his task, Uthman had copies of the authorized version made, and these were distributed to Islamic learning centers in Mecca, Medina, Basra, Damascus, and other cities. All other copies of the Quran were burned so no one could challenge the authorized text.[17]

Unity of Copies

Ironically, Muslims today often argue for the divine nature of the Quran by virtue of the "absolute unity" of copies of the Quran. One Muslim claims that "the Quran is one, and no copy differing in even a diacritical point is met with in one among the four hundred millions of Muslims…A manuscript with the slightest variation in the text is unknown."[18]

Muslims claim the unity of the copies of the Quran is greater than that of any other holy book in existence. We are told, "the Holy Quran is the only divinely revealed Scripture in the history of mankind which has been preserved to the present time in its exact original form."[19] How can such unity be accounted for unless God were behind the Quran?

Diction and Style

Muslims also argue for the divine nature of the Quran by saying that both the style and diction are such that it cannot be man-made. The Quran is said to be the most excellent Arabic poetry and prose ever written or recited in human history.[20] The Quran's beauty is especially a miracle, Muslims claim, in view of the fact that Muhammad was an "unlettered prophet" (that is, he was illiterate).

Changed Lives

Muslims further claim that because the Quran has changed more than a billion people's lives, it is surely divine and not man-made. What human book could bring about such a massive change in the lives of so many people around the world? To Muslims, the incredible growth of Islam is an ironclad proof of the Quran's divine source.

Agreement with Modern Science

Still further, Muslims argue that the agreement of modern science with the Quran proves it is a divine book. Indeed, a book produced in the seventh century could not agree with modern science unless God were behind it, for the Quran states many things that were scientifically unknown in the seventh century.

Prophecy

Some Muslims offer predictive prophecies in the Quran as proof that Muhammad could perform miracles and that the Quran must indeed be a divine book. After all, how could Muhammad prophesy the future without God being involved? For example, Muhammad prophesied that the Muslims would be militarily victorious at home and abroad.

Abrogation

Muslims say that a prerogative of the Quran is *abrogation*, which involves the annulling of a former law by a new law (Sura 16:101). What this means is that Allah is not bound to his revelations. If he wants, he is free to bring new revelation that contradicts former revelation. If need be, Allah is free to rescind earlier revelations and bring about entirely new and different ones.

For example, Muhammad originally ordered his followers to pray toward Jerusalem (Sura 2:150; 2:142). However, when the Jews rejected him and called him an imposter, he received new revelation to the effect that the correct direction of prayer should be toward Mecca (Sura 2:125). This change is in keeping with what we read in Sura 2:106: "If we abrogate a verse or consign it to oblivion, we offer something better than it or something of equal value."

Islamic Tradition

As Islam expanded, many situations arose among Muslims for which the Quran contained no explicit instruction. Muslims eventually began to appeal to traditions about Muhammad's life for the answers. These Muslims believed God directed Muhammad in all he said and did, so they came to depend on traditions regarding the way he lived to guide them in every area of life—personal, social, political, and religious.

Muhammad was widely regarded as the ideal human being and was therefore a model worthy of imitation. During his life, Muhammad had settled many questions, not by divine revelation from Allah but by decisions he made on a case-by-case basis. For this reason his words and actions were recognized, even during his own lifetime, as worthy of imitation. For this reason, his teachings and deeds became fixed in writing and became a standard of behavior alongside the Quran.[21]

Muhammad's teachings and deeds are called the Sunnah ("path") of the prophet, and they are found in numerous collections of the

Hadith ("traditions"), which were compiled over many years. Scholar Gerhard Nehls tells us that "Sunnah and Hadith are technically synonymous terms, but sunnah 'implies the *doings* and *practices* of Muhammad'...It is thus a concrete implementation, a tangible form and the actual embodiment of the Will of Allah."[22]

The Sunnah, found in collections of the Hadith, represents Muhammad's way of acting or thinking in various situations. According to Christi Wilson, the Hadith contains "records of what Muhammad did, what he allowed, and what he enjoined. As such they form a model for conduct and a basis for law."[23] Whenever someone does not find the answers he is looking for in the Quran, he should then consult the Hadith. Muslims believe the Hadith ranks second only to the Quran and is complementary to the Quran. The Hadith helps to explain and clarify the meaning of the Quran and to present it in a more practical form.[24]

Muslims believe that by mimicking the sayings and deeds of Muhammad in their daily lives, they will be more pleasing to Allah. In the Hadith, we find Muhammad engaged in such things as eating, sleeping, mating, planning, praying, traveling, relating to family members and others, going on expeditions, seeking revenge against enemies, and much more.[25] People who pattern their lives after the example of Muhammad stand a greater chance of pleasing Allah and entering paradise.

A CHRISTIAN RESPONSE

Muslims often claim the Quran is divine because "no error, alteration, or variation" has touched its copies since its inception, but this does not accurately reflect the facts. The Quran of today is a nearly perfect copy of its seventh-century counterpart (that is, the seventh-century authorized version produced under Uthman's supervision). But Christians challenge that these copies reflect Muhammad's exact words. Historical sources show that several differing texts circulated in Syria, Armenia, and Iraq prior to the final revision produced by Uthman. Uthman called in Muhammad's long-time secretary, Zaid, to oversee the final and definitive authorized version of the Quran. All other copies of the Quran were then burned so no one could challenge the authorized text.

Alfred Guillaume, perhaps one of the most famous Western scholars on Islam from the non-Islamic world, points out that not all Muslims accepted Uthman's recension, nor are all versions of the Quran identical:

> Only the men of Kufa refused the new edition, and their version was certainly extant as late as A.D. 1000. Uthman's edition to this day remains the authoritative word of God to Muslims. Nevertheless, even now variant readings, involving not only different reading of the vowels but also occasionally a different consonantal text, are recognized as of equal authority one with another.[26]

A simple comparison of different transmitted versions of the Quran reveals variants between them—variants involving letter differences, diacritical differences, and vowel differences. For illustration purposes, consider some transliterated words from the Hafs transmission and the Warsh transmission of the Quran. (The Hafs transmission is used in most parts of the Islamic world, and the Warsh transmission is used in west and northwest Africa.)

- In Sura 2:132 the Hafs transmission has the word *wawassa*. The Warsh transmission has *wa'awsa*.
- In Sura 5:54 the Hafs transmission has the word *yartadda*. The Warsh transmission has *yartadid*.
- In Sura 2:140 the Hafs transmission has the word *taquluna*. The Warsh transmission has *yaquluna*.
- In Sura 20:63 the Hafs transmission has the word *hazayni*. The Warsh transmission has *Inna hazani*.

This sampling of variants demonstrates that the Muslim claim of "perfect unity" in the copies of the Quran is incorrect.[27]

Christian scholars Norman Geisler and Abdul Saleeb point out that even if today's Quran were a perfect copy of Muhammad's original, it still would not prove the original was inspired from God:

All it would demonstrate is that today's Quran is a carbon copy of whatever Muhammad said; it would say or prove nothing about the truth of what he said. The Muslim claim that they have the true religion, because they have the only perfectly copied Holy Book, is as logically fallacious as someone claiming it is better to have a perfect printing of a counterfeit thousand dollar bill than a slightly imperfect printing of a genuine one![28]

Beauty and Eloquence

Though Muslims often argue that the Quran's beauty and eloquence prove the author is God (considering that Muhammad was an "unlettered prophet"), beauty and eloquence are not tests for divine inspiration. If they were, then many other works of art throughout human history would have to be deemed divinely inspired. For example, the musical compositions of Bach, Mozart, and Beethoven, and the writings of Shakespeare and other literary greats, would have to be considered divinely inspired.

One must wonder whether Muslims would accept a challenge to produce a portion of the Quran comparable to any of Shakespeare's writings, or else be willing to accept that his writings are divinely inspired.[29] That may seem a silly challenge, but it is akin to the Muslim challenge to the world to produce a single chapter comparable to a chapter in the Quran.

One fact that seems to argue against the eloquence and beauty of the Quran is that it contains many grammatical errors. Iranian Muslim author Ali Dashti wrote a book—published posthumously—that documented these errors.

> The Quran contains sentences which are incomplete and not fully intelligible without the aid of commentaries; foreign words, unfamiliar Arabic words, and words used with other than the normal meaning; adjectives and verbs inflected without observance of the concord of gender and number; illogical and ungrammatically applied pronouns which sometimes have no referent; and predicates which in rhymed passages are often

remote from the subjects. These and other such aberrations in the language have given scope to critics who deny the Quran's eloquence…To sum up, more than 100 Quranic aberrations from the normal rules and structure of Arabic have been noted.[30]

Fulfilled Prophecy

The fact that the Quran prophesied that Muslims would be victorious at home and abroad (for example, Sura 30:1-5) hardly shows the book is divine. Unlike the Christian Bible, which makes very precise predictions many hundreds of years in advance—for example, precisely predicting that Jesus would be born in Bethlehem (Micah 5:2), that He would be born of a virgin (Isaiah 7:14), and that he would be pierced for man's sins (Zechariah 12:10)—the prediction that Muslims would be militarily victorious is unimpressive, especially considering Muhammad's overwhelming military force.

The prediction of Islamic military victory at home and abroad makes more sense when taken as a prebattle victory speech from Muhammad to boost the morale of his followers, not as a supernatural prediction. It would be much like a leader of an army saying to the troops, "Fight bravely, for we will be victorious!"

> With regard to the victories, it is impossible to prove these to be valid predictions, since the time between prediction and fulfillment was almost nil. We also realize that Mohammed obviously *expected* victory, otherwise he would not have been fighting. Besides that, he also needed to encourage his warriors. In every war that has been fought, both parties have expected and predicted victory. One of the two parties has *always* been right; therefore we cannot regard these predictions as prophecies.[31]

Agreement with Modern Science

The claim that the Quran's agreement with modern science proves its divinity is an unconvincing argument. Foundationally, conformity to modern science is not a proof of divine inspiration. As modern scientists themselves admit, scientific models are constantly changing, so they are not absolute gauges of what is true or false. What was accepted as scientifically true yesterday may not necessarily be accepted as scientifically true tomorrow. Any who doubt that scientific models constantly change should read Thomas Kuhn's book *The Structure of Scientific Revolutions.*

Further, the Quran contains some highly questionable scientific statements, such as the statement that human beings are formed from a clot of blood (Sura 23:14). Certainly no reputable scientist would go along with that statement. Further, Sura 18:86 teaches that the sun sets in a spring of murky water. Obviously, no scientist (or even nonscientist) would entertain such an idea.

Many of the world's greatest scientists have been Christians working from within a Christian worldview—including Nicolaus Copernicus, Johannes Kepler, and Sir Isaac Newton. These brilliant men found to be true what many others have discovered: The Bible is a book that we can trust.

Abrogation

The doctrine of abrogation contradicts the view that the Quran is a divine book. If the Quran on earth is a perfect copy of the eternal Quran on a tablet in heaven in the presence of Allah, authored by almighty God, why the need for changes in the revelation given to Muhammad? Does God change his mind? If God is all-knowing, wouldn't the initial revelation given to Muhammad be final and not need to be changed?

My former colleague Walter Martin suggests that six key theological problems emerge if the doctrine of abrogation is legitimate:

1. We cannot trust the Quran, not only because it has divinely inspired contradictions but because we have no assurance that God will not abrogate again and annul the present revelation.

2. Muslims may argue that future abrogation will not occur because Muhammad was the last prophet, but what if God abrogates that and brings still another prophet?

3. How can we trust God with our eternal souls, knowing He could abrogate His mercy on us?

4. Abrogation involves not only adding new revelation but also contradicting and annulling former revelation. This necessarily means God either changed His mind on a matter, or He was unaware of how future contingent events would turn out and was thus forced to make a change.

5. Abrogation calls into question God's attributes, such as His foreknowledge (He did not have sufficient knowledge to avoid abrogation).

6. If God is inconsistent, what is the basis for morality and ethics? We are left with no absolute right and wrong that serve as a foundation for our ethics.[32]

Many Christians have wondered why Muslims persist in arguing against the veracity of the Bible because of its alleged contradictions while at the same time holding to the doctrine of abrogation in the Quran. Christians have also noted that one verse in the Quran affirms the doctrine of abrogation (Sura 2:106), but another verse says, "No change can there be in the words of God" (Sura 10:64).

Not Eternal

The Quran does not seem to be an eternal book, as Muslims claim. Indeed, if the Quran is eternal, why does it allocate so many words to temporal issues that existed among Muhammad's own family and fellow Muslims? The Suras include a curse against Muhammad's uncle (Sura 111), an admonition to Muhammad's wives to remain subject to him (Sura 33), and words against the elephant brigade of Abraha, the Christian ruler of Abyssinia, who had come up against the Muslims in Mecca (Sura 105). Gleason Archer suggests that the fact that the Quran "is so focused on the lifetime of Muhammad himself strongly suggests that it was actually Muhammad who composed the book himself, rather than it being dictated to him by some angelic spokesman of Allah."[33]

Changed Lives

Though Muslims claim the Quran is divine because it has changed so many lives, the truth is that changed lives are not a proof of divine inspiration. Mormons claim their lives have been changed by the Book of Mormon. Moonies say their lives have been changed by Reverend Moon's *Divine Principle*. Hindus say their lives have been changed by the Vedas.

Any set of ideas that a person puts into practice can have a life-changing effect. But that does not mean God inspired those ideas.

Clearly, the Quran does not enjoy the ironclad proof of divinity Muslims hope for. In fact, the evidence points to the Quran being a man-made book.

Muslim Tradition Unreliable

Scholars believe that many traditions presently contained in the Hadith were deliberately invented 100 to 200 years after the time of Muhammad by various Muslims to support the customs or beliefs of rival parties as divisions arose in Islam. Some portions of the Hadith probably are not based on the life and teachings of Muhammad.

Even some Muslim scholars admit that not all traditions about Muhammad are legitimate. In fact, Muslim scholars have developed methods of sifting through the Hadith to evaluate them, weed out questionable or spurious ones, and preserve authentic ones in systematically arranged collections.[34] Even with these methods, however, scholars have no foolproof way of knowing for sure what is authentic and what is not.

3

MUHAMMAD: THE PROPHET OF ISLAM

ONE OFTEN HEARS Muhammad's name upon the lips of Muslims—something that shows the tremendous respect and even veneration they have for him. Worshippers at Muslim mosques, beggars seeking alms, the sick and the dying, and Muslim soldiers under attack all utter his name. A mother soothes her infant to sleep by singing his name in a cradlesong. Muslims often inscribe his name on the doorposts of their homes. Muhammad is a holy name among Muslims.[1]

THE MUSLIM VIEW OF MUHAMMAD

The Prophetic Backdrop

The Quran says Allah has sent a prophet to every nation to let people know there is only one true God.[2] Islamic tradition claims 124,000 prophets have been sent to humankind.

Each prophet's revelation is said to have been appropriate only for the age in which he lived. When God gives a new book to one of the great prophets, it supersedes the previous books. This means the revelation that came through Muhammad superseded all previous revelations, including the Bible. The previous prophets presented revelation only for their age, but Muhammad's revelation is for all time.[3]

Muslims believe that all of Allah's prophets taught the same basic message—that there is only one true God and that people must submit to his laws and do good works in view of the coming day of judgment.[4] Different prophets may appear to have delivered different messages, but that is due to peoples' distortions of the prophets' fundamentally identical teachings. Even Jesus' words are said to be hopelessly distorted in the New Testament. Jesus' original teachings were supposedly in full agreement with Muhammad's.

Muhammad's Culture

Prior to Muhammad's birth, the Quraysh tribe had come into possession of Mecca, a barren valley, and built a thriving community there. The community flourished as a result of commercial trade, and the Quraysh tribe rapidly emerged as a powerful tribal group. A member of such a tribe enjoyed protection. Should an outsider murder a member, the tribe would avenge him. The fear of blood vengeance by such a tribe served as a powerful deterrent to crime in Arabia.[5]

Muhammad was born into a polytheistic culture. The people believed in many gods and goddesses.[6] They also believed in animism, for in their thinking, they had to appease various spirits, demons, and powers that were associated with rocks, streams, trees, and other parts of nature.

Muhammad's Birth

Muhammad was born in Mecca in AD 570, shortly after the death of his father, who had been a member of the powerful Quraysh tribe. After Muhammad's mother died when he was six years old, his grandfather cared for him briefly, and then his father's brother (Muhammad's uncle), Abu Talib, brought him up.

According to the Quran, Muhammad grew up in poverty (Sura 93:6-7). At first he shared the religious beliefs of his community. As time passed, however, he grew increasingly dissatisfied with the polytheism and animism that permeated his culture. He became uncomfortable with the fact that 360 gods and idols were worshipped within the walls of the *Ka'ba*—the religious black stone shrine in the heart of Mecca.

Muhammad the Merchant

As a young man, Muhammad was of medium height and build and had dark, slightly curly hair and heavy eyebrows. He evidently had rather large extremities—head, hands, and feet—and a black vein that swelled on his forehead whenever he became angry.[7] He was extremely neat, gentle, sincere, amiable, companionable, generous, and shrewd; he disliked strong odors, had a keen insight into human nature, was a good improviser, was undeniably sensual, and could be cruel and vindictive to enemies.[8]

As an adult, Muhammad became apprenticed as a camel boy to a rich widow named Khadija. While under her employ, he showed himself to be honest and trustworthy, and he eventually rose to become the manager of all her trading interests, overseeing caravans on her behalf.

As a merchant, Muhammad often went on lengthy caravan journeys, sometimes going as far as Syria and possibly Egypt. These journeys enabled him to encounter people of different religions and nationalities.[9] He met Christians, Jews, and perhaps Zoroastrians on the trade routes he traveled for the next 15 years. At the same time he observed the degenerate state of the religion and morals of his own people in Mecca.[10] In his encounters with these three religions, he noticed their common teaching about a future judgment in which the righteous would be rewarded, but the wicked would be punished and tormented in hell. This teaching would become a central tenet of Islam.

Muhammad also likely encountered representatives of Christianity and Judaism in Mecca as caravans and merchants visited the city to do business. Unfortunately, the historical evidence suggests that the version of Christianity Muhammad encountered during these years was a particular brand of unorthodox Christianity known as Nestorianism. Its influence on Muhammad appeared when Muhammad later taught that Jesus was not God, that He was not the Son of God, that He was not a Savior or Redeemer, and that He was just a man who was a prophet of God.

Muhammad served Khadija so well that she decided to marry him even though he was 15 years younger than her. Because Khadija was so wealthy, Muhammad no longer had to work for a living. He could now focus his sole attention on spiritual matters and engage in long periods of seclusion and meditation. By all accounts, Muhammad's marriage to Khadija was a happy one.[11]

Khadija had an Ebionite Christian background.[12] Ebionite Christianity denied the deity of Jesus Christ and held that he was a mere man, a prophet who was the natural son of Joseph and Mary. Jesus allegedly distinguished Himself by strict observance of the Jewish law, and He was chosen to be the Messiah because of His legal piety. Jesus' mission as the Messiah was not to save humankind but to call all humanity to obey the law. This is another distorted view of Christianity that would surface in Muhammad's theology.

Muhammad's Revelation

In Muhammad's time, spiritually minded people would commonly retreat once a year to a cave in utter solitude. Muhammad practiced this for several years in a cave in Mount Hira.

Muhammad was meditating when suddenly the angel Gabriel appeared to him and commanded him to "recite" in the name of God. At first Muhammad failed to respond, and the angel seized him by the throat and shook him as he repeated the command to recite. Muhammad again failed to respond, so the angel choked him until he yielded.[13] Muhammad began to recite revelations given to him by the angel.

Muhammad was unsure what to make of this experience. He was concerned that he might be possessed by an evil spirit. Khadija, however, assured him that the source of the revelations was divine.

Concern about the nature of these revelations is understandable. After all, Muhammad received these revelations from the angel in an altered state of consciousness.[14] His body was subject to ecstatic seizures. When he received revelation, his whole body became agitated, his face contorted, perspiration vigorously poured down his face, he heard bells ringing, he fell to the ground and foamed at the mouth, and he roared like a camel.[15]

Eventually, after a period of self-questioning that lasted months, Muhammad finally saw himself as a genuine prophet of Allah. He felt he was a messenger of the one true God already known to Christians and Jews. Muhammad also came to believe that the revelations the earlier prophets received had become corrupted through time and that God had called him to restore God's message to its original purity. Moreover, whereas the former prophets only had an incomplete revelation of Allah, Muhammad was now to bring about Allah's complete and final revelation.[16]

As Allah's prophet, Muhammad was to recite revelations he received from the angel Gabriel. The Arabic word translated *recite* is the word that gives the Quran its title, and it means "the reciting," or "the reading." These revelations to Muhammad continued for 23 years and were later compiled into the Quran, Islam's holy book.

The Quran is often called "the miracle of Muhammad" because of the traditional belief that Muhammad was uneducated and unable to write. He was known as the "unlettered prophet."

Key among the revelations Muhammad received was that Allah is the one true God and that Allah appointed Muhammad himself to be his messenger. Muhammad denounced Mecca's false gods and idolatrous worship, and he preached a strict monotheism. He taught that man is to be Allah's slave, and his first duty to Allah is to submit to and obey him. Muhammad spoke of a terrible future day of judgment in which the righteous would be rewarded with the pleasures of a sensual paradise, but evildoers would be punished in the fires of hell.

Muslim tradition claims that miracles accompanied Muhammad's revelations. For example, Muhammad allegedly fed a multitude of people with a handful of dates, healed blind eyes and other diseases, raised people from the dead, and caused barren fields to yield fruit.[17]

Resistance in Mecca

Muhammad had very few converts at first. In fact, in the three years since his calling as a prophet, he had only 13 followers, including his wife Khadija and some close friends. The number eventually grew to around 40, including people mostly from the poorer classes.

The richer classes did not like Muhammad's message because they felt it interfered with their business. The main source of income in the city came from the many pilgrims who traveled from all over the world to worship the 360 idols in the Ka'ba.[18] If suddenly a prophet branded all the deities in the Ka'ba false, visitors to Mecca would drop dramatically, and the business market would crash. Muhammad obviously made few friends among the businessmen of the city.

As Muhammad was persecuted by such men, he became ever more convinced that he was a true prophet of God, for he was experiencing the same kind of rejection and persecution Moses and Jesus faced. Fortunately, both his wife, Khadija, and his uncle, Abu Talib, had prestige and influence and were able to protect him from attack.

In AD 619, however, Muhammad suffered the loss of both Khadija and Abu Talib. Muhammad found himself without the protection of his clan, and life suddenly became difficult for his Muslim followers.

Migration to Medina

Following Abu Talib's death, the leaders of some of the various tribes in Mecca vowed to assassinate Muhammad. Muhammad became aware of this plot (allegedly through a revelation from Gabriel), and he and 150 followers fled to Yathrib, a city 280 miles north of Mecca, on September 25, AD 622. This migration was so important that it was called the *Hijra* (literally, "emigration"), and the year 622 became the first year of the Muslim calendar and marks the official beginning of Islam.[19]

The people of Yathrib were much more open to monotheism than those in Mecca because many of the town's residents were monotheistic Jews. Muhammad quickly began fulfilling his role as prophet in the new town. He was successful in his leadership, and many of the people in the city became Muslims. He set up a virtual theocracy, combining politics with religion. Muhammad became king and prophet.[20] In honor of Muhammad, the name of the town was changed to Medina—"city of the Prophet."

Not all went according to Muhammad's plans, however. He expected the Jews and Christians to recognize him as one in a long line of prophets and to give allegiance to him. With this in mind, Muhammad initially taught, based on revelation from Allah, that people were to turn toward Jerusalem when praying. Muhammad became bitterly disappointed when Jews and Christians rejected him. Following this, Muhammad's attitude toward both groups shifted dramatically. Through revelation from Allah, the direction of prayer was promptly changed toward Mecca. This marked Muhammad's abandonment of the Jewish-Christian tradition and the beginning of Islam as an independent religion.[21]

In keeping with this, early references to Christians and Jews in the Quran were quite amicable (Sura 2:62,256). Later references became more hostile (Sura 9:5,29).

Though things for the most part began well at Medina, life eventually became difficult for those who migrated from Mecca because they had no money and no valuables. They were on the verge of straining the good graces of the people of Medina. Muhammad promptly received a revelation from Allah which allowed his followers to raid caravans enroute to Mecca, where his enemies lived (Sura 9:74). By raiding caravans headed for Mecca, he greatly aided himself and his followers, and he dealt a blow to his enemies.

Muhammad's movement took on the character of religious militarism. He transformed his followers into fanatical fighters by teaching them that if they died fighting Allah's cause, they would be instantly admitted to paradise. Another motivation for fighting was that the spoils of these caravan raids were divided among Muhammad's men, with Muhammad keeping one-fifth of everything. Not unexpectedly, these caravan raids led to war with the Meccans.

Meanwhile, in the ten years following Khadija's death, Muhammad married another 11 women, though the Quran limits the number of wives a man can marry to four (Sura 4:3). According to Muslim tradition, Muhammad's sexual prowess was legendary (Hadith 1:268).

Many have also noted the impropriety of Muhammad becoming betrothed to a six-year-old girl named Aishah, consummating his marriage to her when she was just nine years old.[22]

Muhammad Takes Mecca

In AD 628, the leaders of the Quraysh tribe in Mecca made a treaty with Muhammad that stipulated that both sides would not fight but would keep the peace for the next ten years. The treaty also stipulated that Muhammad and his followers would be permitted to make pilgrimages to Mecca. However, in January, 630, just two years after signing the treaty, a Meccan murdered a Muslim, and Muhammad attacked Mecca with an overwhelming force of 10,000 men.

The leaders of Mecca surrendered with little resistance, and Muhammad quickly took control of the city, destroying all the idols in the Ka'ba. Because Muhammad gave a general amnesty and later a generous pardon to his former enemies in Mecca, many of them were won over to his side and followed him in future campaigns. The Ka'ba was then made a center for religious pilgrimage.

The Death of the Prophet

Muhammad died suddenly in AD 632, a mere two years after his Meccan conquest. Muhammad had not designated who would become leader should he die, and the process of choosing a new leader caused an ordeal. Some Muslims believed the caliphs should be elected by Islamic leadership (a caliph is a "representative" or "delegate").[23] (This represents the beginning of Sunni Muslims.) Other Muslims believed the successor should be hereditary. (This represents the beginning of Shi'ite Muslims.) Abu Bakr, who had been designated by Muhammad to lead prayers when he was absent, was soon elected by the majority to be the new caliph.

Muslims claim that Muhammad's life and character demonstrate that he was the last and greatest of all the prophets. Moreover, they say, the geometric growth of Islam around the world proves that Muhammad and his religion had divine approval.

A CHRISTIAN RESPONSE

From a biblical perspective, revelations from a new prophet must agree with the revelations of former prophets, assuming all these prophets were genuine spokesmen for the same one true God. We see this principle illustrated by the apostle Paul, who said that "even if we or an angel from heaven should preach a gospel other than the one we preached to you, let him be eternally condemned" (Galatians 1:8). Any teaching that contradicts previous authoritative teaching from God is anathema.

The Bereans knew the critical importance of making sure that new claims to truth be measured against the truth of Scripture. They heard Paul speak in Berea, and they checked everything he said against the Old Testament Scriptures (Acts 17:11). Paul commended them for this practice, for he knew that any revelation communicated through him as an apostle of God must be in agreement with what was previously communicated through Old Testament prophets.

Revelations from Muhammad contradict what we know to be revelation from God (contained in the Christian Bible)—especially on such central doctrines as God, Jesus Christ, and the gospel of salvation—so they do not qualify as revelations from God. Rather, Muhammad falls into the category of a false prophet (Matthew 24:24-25).

Knowledge of Christianity

Muhammad's knowledge of Christian doctrine was inaccurate in many ways. I previously noted that the primary Christians Muhammad came into contact with in his early years were either Nestorians or Ebionites, both of whom held to heretical views of Jesus Christ. Further, Muhammad's knowledge of Christianity was completely based on oral sources and not on a personal study of the Christian Scriptures. Indeed, an Arabic translation of the New Testament did not exist at that time.[24] The New Testament was probably not translated into Arabic until AD 720, a century after Muhammad's time.[25] What Muhammad learned about Christianity was based solely on conversations he had with people during his travels.

Moral Example

Muslims claim Muhammad's life and character demonstrate that he was the last and greatest of all the prophets. Let's examine whether the historical data backs up the claim. In my view, it does not.

- The Quran speaks of Jesus as being sinless, but it makes no such claims about Muhammad. Rather, the Quran speaks of Muhammad's need to ask for forgiveness (Suras 40:55; 48:2).

- The Quran, based on revelation received from Allah, commands that men should have no more than four wives (Sura 4:3). Muhammad, however, married 11 women after the death of his first wife, Khadija—and one of them was only nine years old.

- Muhammad ordered his men to raid caravans and allowed them to keep the booty as long as he was given one-fifth.

- Unlike Jesus, who taught that we should love our enemies (Matthew 5:44), Muhammad ordered executions of some people in Mecca who had formerly opposed him.

- Jesus defended women in New Testament times, but Muhammad ordered the beating of a woman to retrieve information from her.

- Jesus told Peter to put away his sword (Matthew 26:52), but Muhammad was the "prophet of the sword," actively using it for the furtherance of Islam.

Some Muslims respond to this latter point by bringing up the issue of the Crusades, in which Christians themselves used the sword. However, as apologist Robert Morey has pointed out, "It is logically erroneous to set up a parallel between Muslims killing people in *obedience* to the Quran and Christians killing people in *disobedience* to the Bible. While the Quran commands Jihad, the New Testament forbids it."[26]

Rapid Growth: Not a Gauge of Divine Blessing

Islam has certainly grown at a rapid pace, but popularity is not necessarily a sign of God's blessing. Muhammad's movement started slowly and had only 40 converts for the first years of his ministry. Most Meccans rejected his message. Muslims would make a stronger case if they could argue that Islam immediately became immensely popular as soon as it emerged. But that is not what happened. Even if it had happened, that still would not prove blessing by God, for many things throughout history have become popular that were not blessed by God. (Consider how popular unhealthy fast food is today, or the growth of the pornography industry.)

Only after Muhammad sanctioned use of the sword did Islam begin to grow rapidly. This hardly constitutes proof of divine blessing. Certainly many people would rather have become Muslims than be pierced through with a sword.

Christianity grew explosively in the first few centuries after Christ without use of the sword. In fact, the sword was used against the Christians by Roman soldiers, but Christianity still grew! That seems much more of a miracle than Islam's growth.

No True Miracles

Muhammad was not a true miracle worker. Nowhere does the Quran record Muhammad performing any supernatural feats of nature. He explicitly disavowed such ability. When asked why he did not perform miracles as the other prophets did, he responded that the Quran was his miracle (Sura 29:48-50).

Contrary to the Quran, however, the Hadith contains literally hundreds of miracle stories of Muhammad. We have good reason for doubting the veracity of these miracle claims:

- The primary authoritative source for Muslims—the Quran—has no record of such miracles. Rather, it portrays Muhammad refusing to do miracles (Suras 3:181-84; 4:153; 6:8-9). Why should we consider the miracle legends contained in Muslim tradition (the Hadith) authentic when the Quran portrays Muhammad as refusing such miracles? If the Quran has a higher authority for the Muslim than Muslim traditions, why do Muslims give credence to the traditions over the Quran on this matter?

- Most of the individuals who collected miracle stories of Muhammad lived between one and two hundred years after Muhammad's time—they were not eyewitnesses of Muhammad. Two hundred years is plenty of time for miracle legends to develop.

- One must wonder whether some of these miracle stories were invented specifically to answer Christian apologists who tried to show Jesus' superiority because of His miracles.

- Many of these miracle stories seem quite similar to the legendary stories of Jesus contained in the New Testament apocrypha, written long after the time of Jesus. Such accounts are obviously inauthentic when compared to the historically verifiable documents of the New Testament. Because the Muslim traditions bear such strong similarity to the nature of the apocryphal books, their authenticity is every bit as doubtful as the apocryphal books'.

Was Muhammad Illiterate?

Muhammad may not have been an illiterate prophet. According to certain Hadith sources, Muhammad asked for paper and ink to write his will. And when he made a treaty with the Meccans, they refused to concede that he was an apostle of Allah, so he struck out that phrase on the treaty and wrote, "Muhammad, son of Abdullah."[27] Further, one wonders how he could have succeeded as a prosperous businessman without being literate.

Muhammad's Prophetic Confusion

When biblical prophets received revelations from God, they were quite sure He was the source. More than 100 times in the Old Testament alone, we find the prophets beginning their utterances, "Thus saith the LORD" (KJV). They knew they were communicating God's words. God even said to Isaiah, "I have put my words in your mouth"

(Isaiah 51:16). Jeremiah wrote, "Then the LORD reached out his hand and touched my mouth and said to me, 'Now, I have put my words in your mouth'" (Jeremiah 1:9).

By contrast, Muhammad was initially quite unsure as to the source of his revelation. He thought he might be possessed by a demonic spirit. His wife, Khadija, convinced him Allah was speaking through him, and she encouraged him to be obedient to the revelations. This does not sound like a true prophet of God.

Demonic Activity?

My examination of the content of Muhammad's revelations, as well as the manner in which he received them, leads me to conclude that a demon indeed was speaking through him. We know Satan is a great deceiver and that he can mimic angels of light (2 Corinthians 11:14). In this case, he mimicked Gabriel. This is why the Bible exhorts Christians, "Dear friends, do not believe every spirit, but test the spirits to see whether they are from God, because many false prophets have gone out into the world" (1 John 4:1).

John Ankerberg and John Weldon offer this confirmation:

> Muhammad's inspiration and religious experiences are remarkably similar to those found in some forms of spiritism. Shamanism, for example, is notorious for fostering periods of mental disruption as well as spirit-possession. Significantly, Muhammad experienced Shaman-like encounters and phenomena. Further, many authorities have noted that spirit possession frequently leads to the kinds of experiences that Muhammad had.[28]

I take no pleasure in saying a demonic spirit spoke through Muhammad, but this is precisely what the evidence seems to indicate. If I am correct in this assessment, the revelations this spirit gave Muhammad have deceived more than a billion people.

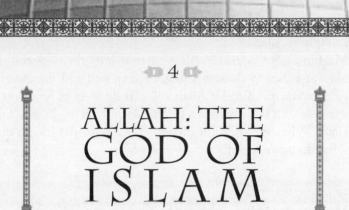

⟪ 4 ⟫

ALLAH: THE GOD OF ISLAM

FOLLOWING THE TERRORIST ATTACK against the World Trade Center and the Pentagon, a Christian minister opened a memorial service with this invocation: "We pray in the name of our God—the God of Christianity, Judaism, and Islam..." Many people—even many Christians in the United States—believe that Christians and Muslims worship the same God. I will demonstrate in this chapter that this is far from the truth.

THE MUSLIM VIEW OF ALLAH

Muslims believe Allah is the only true God. The term *Allah* is probably derived from *al illah*, which means "the god." Allah has seven primary characteristics: He has absolute unity—he is one and not a Trinity (more on this below)—and he is all-seeing, all-hearing, all-speaking, all-knowing, all-willing, and all-powerful.

Allah Has Many Names

The Quran reveals that Allah has many names, including Most Gracious, Most Merciful, the Sovereign, the Source of Peace, the Guardian of Faith, the Preserver of Safety, and the Supreme (Sura

59:22-24). Though he has many names, Muslims most often refer to him simply as Allah.

Muslims often sprinkle Allah's name into their speech. If a Muslim promises to do something, he may well add the qualification *Enshallah*, meaning "If Allah wills." If he sneezes, he might say, "Praise Allah!" If he witnesses a beautiful sight, he might say, "Glory to Allah!" Whatever he might encounter in day-to-day life, he might say, "Thanks be to Allah!"[1]

Allah Is Singularly One

Muslims view Allah as being absolutely one, and he has no partners or associates.

Allah is different from anything man can conceive. For this reason, Muslims often describe Allah using negative terms. For example, Allah is not a spirit. (They say angels are created beings and are spirits, meaning that they have "subtle bodies," and so to say God is a spirit would imply He is a created being, which is blasphemy.)[2] Muslims also say Allah cannot be seen by anyone and that he does not have parts or members. But they also sometimes speak in positive terms, noting that Allah is full of compassion and mercy.

Some Muslims prefer to use the term *unicity* to emphasize Allah's oneness and utter uniqueness.[3] Allah is entirely separate from the creation and is not manifested in any way. Allah's *will* is manifested in the pages of the Quran, but Allah himself is not manifested. He is utterly transcendent. He is so separate and divorced from the creation, and so unified to himself, that he cannot be associated with creation. Any talk of God revealing Himself would compromise His transcendence.

Muslims thus understand God as being beyond virtually every quality and state that belongs to creatures. Allah is inaccessible. We cannot know him in his true nature, for he is beyond us. He is wholly other and totally different. This means that the Allah of the Quran is unknowable. Yet the Quran includes a verse that teaches that Allah is closer to man than his jugular vein (Sura 50:16). Still, Allah does not personally manifest himself to those he is close to.

Not a Trinity

The emphasis on the absolute oneness of Allah is the primary reason Muslims reject the Christian doctrines of the Trinity and Jesus' divinity. They take the phrase "Son of God" quite literally, and they believe it implies that Allah would have had to have a sexual partner in order to beget Christ. This is why Muslims also reject the idea that Allah is a father. In the Muslim mind-set, the term *father* cannot be divorced from the physical realm. To call Allah a father or heavenly father is blasphemous because it amounts to saying Allah had sexual relations to produce a son—Jesus Christ (see Suras 6:101; 19:35).

When Muslims bring up the subject of the Trinity, they typically describe it in terms of tritheism, which espouses the idea of three gods. (The correct viewpoint recognizes one God eternally manifest in three persons.) Muslims thus accuse Christians of worshipping three gods (see Sura 4:171). Muslims often say the doctrine of the Trinity is contradictory—how can something be both three and one at the same time?

A particularly strange idea that often surfaces in discussions of the Trinity with Muslims is the misunderstanding that Christians believe the Trinity is made up of God, Mary, and Jesus (see Sura 5:116). This was apparently the way Muhammad understood the Trinity.

Good and Evil

One of the more controversial aspects of the Muslim view of Allah relates to his absolute sovereignty. The Quran tells us, "God hath power over all things" (Sura 3:165). In the Muslim view, God brings about both good and evil (Suras 32:13; 113:1-2). God can guide men in righteousness, or he can lead them to evil. In some 20 passages of the Quran, Allah is said to lead men astray. Abdiyah Akbar Abdul-Haqq observes, "Even if a person desires to choose God's guidance, he cannot do so without the prior choice of God in favor of his free choice."[4] Everything that happens in the universe, whether good or bad, is foreordained by the unchangeable decrees of Allah. Muslims believe all our thoughts, words, and deeds (good or evil) were foreseen, foreordained, determined, and decreed from all eternity. Everything is irrevocably and fatefully written (Hadith 8:611). One Muslim theologian, Risaleh-i-Barkhawi, goes so far as to say this:

> Not only can he (God) do anything, he actually is the only one who does anything. When a man writes, it is Allah who has created in his mind the will to write. Allah at the same time gives power to write, then brings about the motion of the hand and the pen and the appearance upon paper. All other things are passive, Allah alone is active.[5]

There is thus a very strong strain of fatalism in Islam. Devout Muslims frequently say *Enshallah*—"If Allah wills."[6] This strong sense of fatalism can lead to irresponsible actions. For example, some children in apartment buildings in Teheran, Iran, fall over low balcony railings to their deaths. Because of the belief that this must have been the will of Allah, authorities do nothing to heighten the railings to prevent such tragedies in the future.[7] Fatalism thus leads to a diminished sense of moral responsibility.

Some Muslims try to explain this contradiction in Allah (causing both good and evil) as relating not to his *nature* but rather to his *will*. However, such an explanation seems less than satisfactory in view of the fact that actions that stem from a will are rooted in a person's nature. As apologists Norman Geisler and Abdul Saleeb put it, "Salt water does not flow from a fresh stream."[8]

One cannot help but notice that the Allah of the Quran seems to act quite arbitrarily. He can choose good, but he can just as easily choose evil. He can choose mercy, but he might just as easily choose severity. He could choose love, but he could just as easily choose hate (see Sura 11:118-19).

So the Quran teaches that Allah engages in both good and evil, and therefore we should not be surprised that the Quran never suggests that Allah is holy. The Quran seems to emphasize Allah's power rather than his purity, his omnipotence rather than his holiness.

Allah Loves, but Only to an Extent

A Muslim cannot truthfully say that God is love the same way a Christian can (1 John 4:16). The Quranic view is that Allah loves those who love him and serve him, but he does not love unbelievers. Allah is merciful to those who do good, but he withholds mercy from evildoers (Suras 2:135; 3:31; 19:96).

One should note that the Islamic version of God's mercy is much different from that of Christianity. Former Muslims Ergun Mehmet Caner and Emir Fethi Caner note that in Islam, "Allah is merciful because he did not kill me or leave me in peril."[9] In contrast, Christian mercy is rooted in God's grace—His unmerited favor.

A CHRISTIAN RESPONSE

Contrary to the Muslim viewpoint, the Bible reveals that God is a highly personal being, and we can establish and enjoy intimate personal relationships with Him. A person is a conscious being—he thinks, feels, purposes, and carries these purposes into action. A person engages in active relationships with others. You can talk to a person and get a response from him. You can share feelings and ideas with him. You can argue with him, love him, and even hate him if you so choose. Surely, by this definition God must be understood as a person.

As inscrutable as this may seem to the human mind, our personal God specially constructed man with a capacity to know and fellowship with Him (Genesis 1:26-27). Our purpose—indeed, our highest aim in life—must be to know God.

Recall that when God created Adam, He declared Adam's loneliness to be "not good" (Genesis 2:18). God made man as a social being. He did not create man to be alone. He created man to enter into and enjoy relationships with others. Man's most important relationship is with God Himself. The human heart knows a hunger that none but God can satisfy, a vacuum that only God can fill. God created us with a need for fellowship with Him, and we are restless and insecure until this becomes our living experience.

People in biblical times undoubtedly knew God intimately in their personal experience. In fact, knowing God was believers' main business in ancient times. We read that Enoch and Noah walked with God (Genesis 5:24; 6:9). God spoke directly (not through an angel) to Noah (Genesis 6:13), Abraham (Genesis 12:1), Isaac (Genesis 26:24), Jacob (Genesis 28:13), Moses (Exodus 3:4), Joshua (Joshua 1:1), Gideon (Judges 6:25), Samuel (1 Samuel 3:4), David (1 Samuel 23:9-12), Elijah (1 Kings 17:2-4), and Isaiah (Isaiah 6:8). Likewise, in the New Testament, God spoke to Peter, James, and John (Mark 9:7), to Philip (Acts 8:29), to Paul (Acts 9:4-6), and to Ananias (Acts 9:10). How different this is from the utterly remote Allah of Islam.

God Is Spirit

Contrary to Islam, which says God is not a Spirit, the Bible informs us that God is indeed Spirit (John 4:24). Because God is a Spirit, He is invisible (Colossians 1:15; 1 Timothy 1:17). John 1:18 tells us, "No one has ever seen God [the Father], but God the One and Only [Jesus Christ], who is at the Father's side, has made him known." When Jesus became a man, He became a visible revelation of the invisible God.

Islam is incorrect in asserting that the suggestion that God is Spirit implies He is a created being, like angels. Scripture indicates that God is Spirit, but He is also eternal. God is an eternal spirit. God is the King eternal (1 Timothy 1:17) who alone is immortal (6:16). God is the "Alpha and the Omega" (Revelation 1:8) and is the first and the last (see Isaiah 44:6; 48:12). God exists "from eternity" (Isaiah 43:13 NASB) and "from everlasting to everlasting" (Psalm 90:2).

God Is Transcendent and Immanent

The theological phrase *transcendence of God* refers to God's otherness or separateness from the created universe and from humanity. The phrase *immanence of God* refers to God's active presence within the creation and in human history (though all the while remaining distinct from the creation). Allah is portrayed as radically transcendent, but the God of the Bible is portrayed as both transcendent and immanent. He is high above His creation but also intimately involved among His creatures.

Deuteronomy 4:39 says, "Acknowledge and take to heart this day that the LORD is God in heaven above and on the earth below." In Isaiah 57:15 God affirms, "I live in a high and holy place, but also with him who is contrite and lowly in spirit." In Jeremiah 23:23-24 God says, "Am I only a God nearby...and not a God far away?" Clearly, God is above and beyond the creation, yet He is simultaneously active in the midst of the creation.

God Reveals Himself

Muslims believe that the Quran manifests Allah's will, but Allah himself is never manifested. Contrary to this viewpoint, the Bible is clear that God has always been the aggressor in making Himself (not just His laws) known. He has always taken the initiative in revealing Himself to humankind. He does this through revelation.

Revelation makes good sense. God is our Father. No loving parent would ever deliberately keep out of his or her child's sight so that the child grew up without knowing of the parent's existence. Such an action would be the height of cruelty. Likewise, for God to create us and then not communicate with us would be a cruel act of abandonment.

God has revealed Himself in two ways—through *general* revelation and *special* revelation. General revelation is available to all persons of all times. For example, God reveals Himself in the world of nature (Psalm 19). Special revelation is God's very specific and clear revelation in such things as His mighty acts in human history (as in the book of Exodus), the person of Jesus Christ (Hebrews 1:2-3), and His message spoken through Old Testament prophets and New Testament apostles (2 Timothy 3:16-17). God delights in making Himself known!

God Is a Trinity

Muslims sometimes come right out and ask, "Do you believe in the Trinity?" This is where the Christian must be cautious. As Sobhi Malek points out, if the Christian simply says, "Yes, I believe in the Trinity," and does not clarify what he means, the Muslim will conclude that the Christian believes in three gods, which is anathema to the Muslim. Yet if the Christian says, "No, I do not believe in the Trinity," he will be in denial of one of the basic doctrines of Christianity.[10] So if a Muslim asks this question, the Christian must give a qualified yes—that is, the Christian must clearly define what the term *Trinity* means.

Muslims typically reject the doctrine of the Trinity for several reasons. Primarily, the doctrine implies that God has partners, an idea Muslims interpret to be heinous. Beyond this, Muslims point out that the word *Trinity* is not in the Bible. Of course, the Muslim term for God's unity *(tawhid)* is not in the Quran either.[11] Yet Muslims believe in the concept of God's unity because they believe the whole of the Quran teaches it. Likewise, though the word *Trinity* is not mentioned in the Bible, the concept is clearly derived from Scripture.

The Christian doctrine of the Trinity is based on (1) evidence that there is only one true God, (2) evidence that three persons are God, and (3) scriptural indications for three-in-oneness within the Godhead. Let's briefly consider these three doctrinal planks:

Evidence for one God. The fact that there is only one true God is the consistent testimony of Scripture from Genesis to Revelation—something you will want to emphasize to your Muslim acquaintance, who probably thinks the Trinity includes three gods. God's oneness is emphasized throughout the Old Testament (Deuteronomy 6:4; 32:39; 2 Samuel 7:22; Psalm 86:10; Isaiah 37:20; 43:10; 44:6; 45:5,14,21-22; 46:9) as well as the New Testament (John 5:44; 17:3; Romans 3:29-30; 16:27; 1 Corinthians 8:4; Galatians 3:20; Ephesians 4:6; 1 Thessalonians 1:9; 1 Timothy 1:17; 2:5; James 2:19; 1 John 5:20-21; Jude 25).

Evidence for three persons who are called God. Though Scripture is clear there is only one God, God's revelation to humankind also clearly refers to three distinct persons who are called God. Be sure to emphasize that the three persons are not God, Jesus, and Mary, but rather the Father, Jesus, and the Holy Spirit.

Scripture calls each of these three persons God—the Father (1 Peter 1:2), Jesus (Hebrews 1:8), and the Holy Spirit (Acts 5:3-4). Each person of the Trinity individually possesses the attributes of deity, including omnipresence (Psalm 139:7; Matthew 19:26; 28:18), omniscience (Romans 11:33; Matthew 9:4; 1 Corinthians 2:10), and omnipotence (Matthew 28:18; Romans 15:19; 1 Peter 1:5). As well, each of the three performs works of deity. For example, all three were involved in the creation of the universe: the Father (Genesis 2:7; Psalm 102:25), Jesus (John 1:3; Colossians 1:16; Hebrews 1:2), and the Holy Spirit (Genesis 1:2; Job 33:4; Psalm 104:30).

Scriptural indications for three-in-oneness. Scripture indicates there are three persons in the one God. Perhaps one of the best verses is Matthew 28:19. After Jesus had risen from the dead, He referred to all three persons of the Trinity while instructing the disciples: "Therefore go and make disciples of all nations, baptizing them in the name of the Father and of the Son and of the Holy Spirit." The word *name* is singular in the Greek, pointing to one God, but the Godhead includes three distinct persons—the Father, the Son, and the Holy Spirit.

Paul's benediction in his second letter to the Corinthians gives further evidence for God's three-in-oneness: "May the grace of the Lord Jesus Christ, and the love of God [the Father], and the fellowship of the Holy Spirit be with you all" (2 Corinthians 13:14). This verse shows the intimacy that each of the three persons has with the believer.

As you try to share the correct view of the Trinity with your Muslim acquaintance, he might say the doctrine does not make sense. How can three be one? Help your friend see that the Trinity does not involve three gods in one god, nor does it involve three persons in one person. Those kinds of statements would be illogical. But the Trinity involves one God who is eternally manifest in three persons (one What, three Whos). The Trinity may not be easy to understand, but we should not be surprised that finite minds cannot fully comprehend the nature of an infinite God. Scholar Dean Halverson notes that "the difficulty of understanding and explaining the concept of the Trinity is, in fact, evidence for its divine origin. It is unlikely that such a concept would be invented by mere humans."[12]

God Is Love

While "Allah loveth not those that do wrong" (Sura 3:140), the

Christian Bible tells us that "God demonstrates his own love for us in this: While we were still sinners, Christ died for us" (Romans 5:8). God loves all sinners (John 3:16; Romans 5:1-10).

God is not just characterized by love. He is the very personification of love (1 John 4:8). Love permeates His being. And God's love does not depend on the lovability of the object (human beings). God loves us despite the fact that we are fallen in sin (John 3:16). First John 4:9-10 tells us, "This is how God showed his love among us: He sent his one and only Son into the world that we might live through him. This is love: not that we loved God, but that he loved us and sent his Son as an atoning sacrifice for our sins."

God Is Holy

Unlike the Allah of the Quran, the God of the Bible is holy. This means not only that He is entirely separate from all evil but also that He is absolutely righteous (Leviticus 19:2). He is pure in every way. God is separate from all that is morally imperfect. The Scriptures lay great stress upon this attribute of God (Exodus 15:11; 1 Samuel 2:2; Psalm 99:9; 111:9; Isaiah 6:3; Revelation 15:4).

God Is Singularly Good, Just, and Righteous

A key emphasis in the Bible relates to the absolute unity of God's moral character. By *unity*, I mean that God does not have within His nature dualistic ideas of good and evil, mercy and cruelty. God is singularly good, just, and righteous. The God of the Bible abhors evil, does not create evil, and does not lead men astray.

Christian apologists have noted that in Islamic teaching, Allah is not essentially good but is only called good because he does good. He is named for his actions. This line of thinking has an obvious fatal flaw. If Allah is called good because he does good, should we call Allah evil because he also does evil? This conclusion seems difficult to avoid.

If Allah does evil, doesn't this reveal something about his nature? Doesn't an effect resemble its cause? As Thomas Aquinas pointed out, one cannot produce what one does not possess. The inescapable conclusion is that evil is a part of Allah's nature.

Contrary to Islam, the Bible teaches that both good and evil cannot stem from one and the same essence (God). We read that God is light, and "in Him is no darkness at all" (1 John 1:5; compare with Habakkuk 1:13; Matthew 5:48). The Scriptures clearly portray God as singularly good (Psalm 25:8; 31:19; 34:8; 100:5; 106:1; Nahum 1:7), singularly righteous (Ezra 9:15; Psalm 11:7; 33:5; 89:14; Jeremiah 12:1), and singularly just (Genesis 18:25; Psalm 11:7; John 17:25; Hebrews 6:10).

God Is Sovereign, but He Allows for Free Will

The biblical God is absolutely sovereign—He rules the universe, controls all things, and is Lord over all (Psalm 50:1; 66:7; 93:1; Isaiah 40:17; 1 Timothy 6:15). At the same time, Scripture portrays man as having a free will (Genesis 3:1-7). Man's finite understanding cannot comprehend how both divine sovereignty and human free will can both be true, but Scripture teaches both doctrines. In fact, they are often side by side in a single Scripture verse (see Acts 2:23; 13:48). This means that the true God, unlike Allah, cannot be held responsible for people's evil choices.

An Objective Basis for Forgiveness

According to the Bible, humankind's dilemma of falling "short of the glory of God" (Romans 3:23) required a solution. Man's sin—his utter unrighteousness—prevented him from coming into a relationship with God on his own. God solved this seemingly insurmountable problem by declaring righteous all those who believe in Jesus. Because of Christ's work on the cross—taking our place and bearing our sins—God acquits believers and pronounces a verdict of not guilty. Romans 3:24 tells us that God gives His "declaration of righteousness" to believers "freely by his grace." The word *grace* literally means "unmerited favor." Because of God's unmerited favor, believers are freely "declared righteous" before God.

Here is the important thing I want to emphasize: God's declaration of righteousness has an objective basis. God did not subjectively decide to overlook man's sin or wink at his unrighteousness. That would be unjust and unrighteous. Instead, Jesus died on the cross for us. He died in our stead and paid for our sins. He ransomed us from death by His own death on the cross.

By contrast, Islam has no atonement, so Allah has no objective basis to forgive sins. This means that Allah's forgiveness is unrighteous and unjust. Only through the cross could God remain just and the justifier of the ungodly who trust in Jesus. To imagine that God can righteously forgive sinners without requiring any atonement "is to impute immorality to God and make him a protector of sin rather than its condemner."[13]

The Biblical God Is Not Allah

Though many people think the Allah of Islam and the God of the Bible are one and the same, the Bible compels us to reject this line of thinking. The differences are so substantive that a common identity is impossible:

The God of the Quran	The God of the Bible
is a radical unity (Sura 4:171)	is a Trinity (Matthew 28:19)
cannot have a son (Suras 6:101; 19:35)	has an eternal Son named Jesus Christ (John 3:16)
is not spirit	is Spirit (John 4:24)
is wholly transcendent (Sura 4:171)	is both transcendent and immanent (Deuteronomy 4:39; Isaiah 57:15; Jeremiah 23:23-24)
brings about both good and evil (Sura 11:118-119)	never engages in evil (1 John 1:5)
is not a father (Suras 19:88-92; 112:3)	is a Father (Matthew 6:9)
loves only those who love and obey him	loves all people, including all sinners (Luke 15:11-24)

reveals only his laws and not himself	has revealed Himself from the beginning (Isaiah 65:1)
has no objective basis for forgiving people (Suras 39:7; 23:102-103)	forgives on the objective basis of Jesus Christ's death on the cross (Romans 3:23-26)

MUSLIMS'
FIVE PRIMARY
DUTIES

ISLAM INVOLVES BOTH BELIEFS (the five doctrines of Islam, which have to do with God, angels, holy books, prophets, and a future judgment) and obligations (the five pillars of Islam). These five pillars *(Arkan-al-Islam)* constitute the five most important acts for a Muslim. All devout Muslims dutifully perform them to please Allah.

These pillars are intended to increase a Muslim's faith and make him or her a better person. Practicing the external motions without any heartfelt commitment is considered meaningless. Such a person will not be saved. However, the person who performs these five pillars and remains steadfastly in the faith of Islam increases his hope that he might make it to *Jannah* (paradise).

My goal in this chapter is to briefly summarize these five religious duties.

1. CREEDAL RECITATION

Muslims sometimes point to a single verse in the Quran that summarizes the Islamic faith: "O ye who believe! Believe in Allah and His messenger and the Scripture which He hath revealed unto His messenger, and the Scripture which He revealed aforetime. Whoso disbelieveth in Allah and His angels and His scriptures and His messengers and the Last Day, he verily hath wandered far astray"

(Sura 4:136). An even more concise statement of faith, however, is the Muslim creed.

Muslims are expected to publicly and daily recite the Muslim creed—the *Shahadah* (literally, "to bear witness"). The creed simply reads, "There is no god but Allah and Muhammad is the Prophet of Allah." Muslim literature often affirms that the reciting of this creed makes one a Muslim. As we saw earlier, however, a mere mechanical reciting of the words is not sufficient to make one a Muslim. Worshippers must meet six conditions: (1) They must repeat the creed aloud, (2) they must understand it perfectly, (3) they must believe it in their hearts, (4) they must profess it until they die, (5) they must recite it correctly, and (6) they must profess and declare it without hesitation.[1]

The creed is the first thing parents whisper into a baby's ears when he or she is born into the world. Muslims seek to have these words upon their lips just prior to the moment of death.[2] If not, someone close to them may utter the words for them.

Scholar Jamal Elias has noted that reciting just the first half of the creed—"There is no God but Allah"—makes one a monotheist, but not necessarily a Muslim. After all, the Arabic word for "God" is "Allah," and a person who says in Arabic that there is one God may just be asserting that he is a monotheist. However, Elias notes, the second half of the recitation—"Muhammad is the Prophet of Allah"—distinguishes Muslims from all other monotheists.[3]

2. PRAYERS

Muslims are expected to perform *salat,* or offer prayers, five times a day: at dawn, noon, afternoon, evening, and night. Such prayers are compulsory for everyone over the age of ten. These prayers include specific words and a series of postures (standing, kneeling, hands and face on the ground, and so forth) while facing Mecca, the holy city for Muslims.[4] The prayers are recited in Arabic and contain the following words:

> God is most great…holiness to thee, oh God, and praise
> to thee…I seek refuge with God from the curse of Satan…

God hears him who praises him…Oh God, have mercy on Muhammad and on his descendants, as thou didst have mercy on Abraham and his descendants…Oh God our Lord, give us the blessings of this life and also the blessings of the life to come, save us from the torments of fire…The peace and mercy of God be with you.[5]

In Muslim parts of the world, at the time for prayer, a strong-voiced man called a *muezzin* will climb up a tower—a *minaret*—and cry out a call for prayer—the *adhan*. He says, "God is great. There is no God but God, and Muhammad is the messenger of God. Come to prayer. Come to prayer. Come to success in this life and the hereafter."[6]

When Muslims hear this call to prayer, they pause from whatever they are doing—whether relaxing at home or working in an office—and engage in the prescribed prayer.[7] In urban areas, a public address system often signals the beginning of prayer.[8] Worshippers may pray at home, at work, or even outdoors as long as the place of prayer is free from distractions and is clean. A Muslim man's prayers can be rendered ineffective if, during the prayer, a dog, a donkey, or a woman passes in front of him (Hadith 1:490).

Muslims are required to wash themselves (hands, face, and feet) in a prescribed manner before praying. This is called *ablution* or *wudu*.[9] Former Muslims Ergun Mehmet Caner and Emir Fethi Caner describe the steps Muslims must take to prepare themselves for prayer:

- wash the hands up to the wrist three times
- rinse out the mouth three times
- clean the nostrils by sniffing water three times
- wash the face from forehead to chin and from ear to ear
- wash the forearms up to the elbows three times
- pass a wet hand over the whole of the head
- wash the feet up to the ankles three times, the right and then the left[10]

If someone passes gas after the cleansing ritual, he must repeat it. Such is the strictness of Islamic law.[11]

For Muslims who work in corporate America—particularly in situations where few others in the office are sympathetic to Muslim religious practices or during travel—engaging in such regular prayer can be a challenge. These Muslims often shorten or combine their prayers, depending on their circumstances. They also carry "Mecca finders"—compasses with the coordinates for Mecca.[12] For Muslims who want to get the most mileage out of their prayers, however, Muslim tradition assures us that prayer inside a Muslim mosque is much more effective—by 25 times—than prayer offered anywhere else.

3. GIVING ALMS

Muslims are expected to give alms *(zakat)* to the Muslim community that amount to one-fortieth (2.5 percent) of one's income. *Zakat*, which literally means "to be pure," signifies the purifying of one's soul.[13] The offering benefits widows, orphans, and the sick, or it can be used to further Islam (for example, to build mosques and religious schools). Giving to charity is considered an extremely meritorious act in Islam (see Suras 24:56; 57:18). Believers give with the conscious awareness that all things ultimately belong to Allah and that each person is a mere trustee for a limited time on earth.[14]

Muslim tradition affirms that Allah withholds his blessing from those who withhold alms (Hadith 2:515). Tradition also indicates that one can nullify salvation by withholding charity (Hadith 2:486). "Save yourself from Hell-fire even by giving half a date-fruit in charity" (Hadith 2:498). Muhammad said almsgiving was important because society is like a body with many parts. If one part of the society suffers, all of society suffers, and so the other parts of society rally in response.[15]

Different Muslim communities handle charity in different ways. In some communities each Muslim makes a charitable contribution to the cause of his choice—generally a local charity. Some Muslims give to their local mosque or to a respected Islamic leader, who then applies the funds to good use. Other Muslim communities have a *zakat* tax collected by the government. The income derived from this tax is then used either for social benefit (building schools, for example) or for religious purposes.

Students of Islam have long noted that Muhammad himself was once poor and was an orphan. Surely this helped promote Islam's emphasis on giving charitably to the poor.

4. RAMADAN

Muslims are expected to fast during the month of Ramadan, the ninth month of the Muslim lunar year. Because the Muslim calendar is based on the lunar year, the month sometimes falls during the winter and sometimes during summer.

During this month, Muslims abstain from food, drink, smoking, and sexual relations during the daylight hours. As soon as there is enough light to distinguish a white thread from a black thread each morning, the fast begins.[16] After sundown—when believers cannot distinguish the threads—they are allowed to partake of these things again until sunrise the next morning.

Understandably, engaging in this fast is easier if one is wealthy enough to stay home and perhaps sleep more during the day. But for those who work during the daylight hours, the fast can quickly exhaust one's stamina and mental drive.[17] In any event, the fast is intended to purify body and soul and increase one's self-awareness.[18] The fast can also yield the forgiveness of sins. Muslim tradition affirms, "Whoever observes fasts during the month of Ramadan out of sincere faith, and hoping to attain Allah's rewards, then all his past sins will be forgiven" (Hadith 1:37).

The month of Ramadan is important to Muslims because they believe Muhammad received the initial revelation of the Quran during this month. Muhammad himself fasted during this sacred time, so in honor of the Prophet, Muslims do so as well.[19]

Muslims are excused from this fast if they are sick, very young or old, mothers of nursing infants, travelers, or insane.

Islam scholar William Miller reports that some Muslims are so strict with this fast that they won't even swallow their own saliva during the daylight hours. They also believe that if even a drop of water goes down their throat while cleaning their teeth, they are required to atone for this slip by keeping another fast.[20] Other Muslims are not so strict. These Muslims are more concerned about avoiding a deliberate breaking of the fast—eating a meal or engaging in sexual relations. Scholar Frederick Denny points out that a deliberate breaking of the fast carries a penalty of having to "fast sixty days, to feed sixty people the equivalent of one meal each, or to give charity equal to a meal to sixty persons. This penalty is known as *kaffara*, meaning 'reparation, penance.'"[21]

Most Muslim families get up early enough to eat a substantial breakfast before the sun rises—one intended to last the day. In Muslim communities, the fast begins with the blast of a siren or perhaps the beating of a drum. During the daytime hours, many restaurants close for business. Some, however, stay open to serve non-Muslims. Some Muslim communities are so strict that they prohibit all eating or drinking in public during the fast. At the end of the day, after the sun has gone down, Muslim families often sit down to a rather elaborate meal. Interestingly, Muslim communities sell more food during the month of Ramadan than any other month of the year.[22]

5. THE PILGRIMAGE TO MECCA

Every Muslim is expected to make an official pilgrimage to Mecca *(Hajj)* at least once in his or her life. A woman may go on the *Hajj* only with her husband's permission, and even then she must be under the protection of a guardian. Going on this pilgrimage is meritorious and greatly enhances one's chances for salvation.[23] The journey cleanses the soul and wipes away sin. Muhammad allegedly said that those who perform the *Hajj* properly "will return as a newly born baby [free of all sins]."[24] The pilgrimage is an exciting time for a Muslim, for he has prayed toward Mecca his entire life, and now he has the chance to go there.

The *Hajj* actually begins before the pilgrim leaves for Mecca during the month of the pilgrimage. Islam scholar Abdulkader Tayob explains:

> The hajj begins at home, where preparations have to be made for the journey...Before the actual departure, a pilgrim visits family and friends and seeks their forgiveness for both known and unintentional acts that may have transpired between them. The pilgrim is getting ready to stand in front of God, and does not want that encounter to be sullied by less than perfect human relations. A perfect pilgrimage leads to complete absolution of sins, and nobody would want to mar such an expectation by neglecting to resolve inter-human friction.[25]

Making the pilgrimage taxes one's health and finances. A Muslim who is unable to go for health reasons may have another person make the *Hajj* for him as proxy. Expenses include not only the pilgrimage to Mecca but also the care of loved ones left behind. The trip is costly, so Muslims may save money for many years to make the trip. Borrowing money to pay for the trip is not wise because the *Hajj* does not become valid until all debts are paid off.

Throughout the entire pilgrimage, Muslims repeatedly recite the *talbiya:* "I am here, O my God, I am here! I am here, Thou art without any associate, I am here! Praise and blessing belong to Thee, and Power."[26] As the pilgrims make their way to the holy precincts of Mecca, they go through gates or checkpoints—*miqats*—beyond which non-Muslims are not permitted to go.[27] As they enter the sacred mosque in Mecca, they recite verses from the Quran, especially Sura 17:80-81:

> Say: "O my Lord! Let my entry be by the Gate of Truth and Honor, and likewise my exit by the Gate of Truth and Honor; and grant me from Thy Presence an authority to aid (me)." And say: "Truth has (now) arrived, and Falsehood perished: for Falsehood is (by its nature) bound to perish."

Once in Mecca, all pilgrims go through the same basic rituals. They start at the Black Stone—12 inches in diameter—which is embedded at the southeast corner of the Ka'ba (religious shrine), and then they run around the building seven times, three times fast and four times slow, counterclockwise. According to Muslim tradition, Abraham, Ishmael, and Muhammad all circled the Ka'ba in this way. This event is known as *tawaf.* Each time pilgrims go around the building, they pause at the southeast corner in order to kiss the Black Stone. If a huge crowd of Muslims is there, they can simply touch the stone with their hand, or perhaps with a stick. If even that proves difficult, one can simply observe the stone and meditate upon it.[28] This ritual yields a blessing from heaven.

Muslims say the Black Stone they worship fell from heaven in the days of Adam.[29] They also believe it is the site of God's covenant with Abraham and Ishmael, so it carries great religious significance.

One highly relevant factor regarding the *Hajj* is that everyone participating in the rituals is dressed the same way. They all wear white garments called *ihram.* This similar attire serves to eliminate all class or status distinctions during the pilgrimage. The rich and the poor are on equal footing.

Other events take place during the pilgrimage. Muslims visit a number of sacred sites, tombs of Muslim saints, and sites containing the relics of Muhammad (this can take a week).[30] Visiting such places increases one's merit before Allah on the day of judgment.[31] Those who successfully complete the pilgrimage are given the title of *Hajji* and look forward to receiving a reward from Allah for visiting the sacred sites.

Not unexpectedly, massive organization and planning is necessary for the Saudi Arabian government to accommodate up to two million pilgrims participating in the same rituals over the space of a few days. These pilgrims pour into the area from Algeria, Afghanistan, Java, Syria, Pakistan, the Sudan, Europe, America, Africa, and other countries. They come by camel, car, bus, train, ship, and plane. The Saudi Arabian government has invested a fortune in building highways, tunnels, and galleries to make things run as smoothly as possible.[32]

Saudi Arabia considers itself the caretaker of Mecca, Islam's holiest city. No Christian churches can be built on its soil, and no Christian missionaries are allowed to enter it.[33]

THE MUSLIM HOPE

These five religious duties—reciting the creed, prayer five times daily, giving alms, fasting during the month of Ramadan, and going on a pilgrimage to Mecca—are extremely meaningful and significant to Muslims. All Muslims are acutely aware, however, that even if they faithfully perform these duties, they still do not have an assurance of going to paradise at death. They can only hope.

⬩ 6 ⬩

ALLAH AND SALVATION

THE PURPOSE OF MAN, according to Islam, is not to know God and become more conformed to His character. Rather, man's purpose is simply to understand God's will and become more obedient to His commands. Salvation is found in complete surrender to Allah. This is in keeping with the meaning of *Islam* ("submission") and *Muslim* ("one who submits"). Salvation, then, is ultimately based on works.

Before we can properly understand the Muslim view of salvation, however, we first need to understand what Islam teaches about sin. Christian scholars have long recognized that a weak view of sin will always lead to a weak view of salvation. Whoever does not recognize a serious sin problem for human beings will generally minimize the need for an atonement. This is true in the religion of Islam.

THE MUSLIM VIEW OF SALVATION

Sin

Islam minimizes the reality of human sin. Muslims firmly deny the Christian doctrine of original sin, which is rooted in the fall of Adam.

To be sure, Muslims concede that Adam disobeyed God and was

evicted from the Garden of Eden. When Adam sinned, however, his nature did not change at all. He did not gain a "sin nature" that would in the future lure him into sinful activity. Adam was the same after his fall as he was before. He was still perfectly able to obey God.

Muslims also believe Adam's fall had no effect on his descendants. Like Adam, his descendants have always been able to obey God as long as they understand what God requires of them. This is why Allah has sent so many prophets to humankind throughout history.

Muslim writer Badru Kateregga affirms that all people are born innocent, pure, and free: "There is no single act which has warped the human will."[1] Muslim tradition records what Muhammad allegedly said on this subject: "No child is born except in the state of natural purity *(fitra)* and then his parents make him Jewish, Christian, or Magian."[2] Another Muslim writer notes that "people are born innocent and remain so until each makes him or herself guilty by a guilty deed. Islam does not believe in 'original sin'; and its Scripture interprets Adam's disobedience as his own personal misdeed—a misdeed for which he repented and which God forgave."[3]

A key argument Muslims offer in support of the idea that Adam did not commit a major sin is that he was a prophet of Allah, and Allah's prophets simply do not engage in major sin. God would never entrust important revelation to one who was an evildoer. Instead of saying that Adam engaged in a major sin, Muslims say Adam just made a mistake, for he forgot God's command not to eat of the tree. He goofed, but then he repented, and all was well.

All of this is not to say that Muslims have no doctrine of sin at all. They do believe sin exists, but they believe people commit sins not because they have a sin nature but because of human weakness and forgetfulness (Sura 4:28). Human beings are easily led astray. They have an inherent feebleness. That is why people need Allah's laws. If sin emerges as a result of forgetfulness and feebleness, Allah's law serves as a constant reminder of what is expected of humankind.

Atonement Unnecessary

The idea that almighty Allah could be bothered by the trifling mistakes of a mere mortal is considered absurd to Muslims. They believe Allah can easily choose to forgive if he so wishes.

Muslims also believe people are able, in their own strength, to free themselves from bondage to sin and choose to follow the path of Allah. Accordingly, an atonement for sin is unnecessary. Muslims do not believe human beings need to be redeemed, and they see no need for the sacrificial death of a Savior (Jesus Christ). They believe man is fundamentally good, and the Muslim hope is anchored in the belief that Allah will forgive those who seek to obey His will.

Another reason an atonement is unnecessary in Muslim theology is that Allah makes his own sovereign (seemingly arbitrary) decisions on matters of salvation. According to the Quran, Allah can lead people on the correct path, or he may lead them astray. Allah can show mercy to people if he wants, or he may show cruelty to them. He is answerable to no one. Because Allah can forgive whomever he wants and condemn whomever he wants, an atonement is entirely unnecessary.

Good Works Are Enough

The Quran teaches that a person's hope of salvation is based on pleasing Allah by good works. We read in Sura 23:102-103: "In the day of judgment, they whose balances shall be heavy with good works, shall be happy; but they, whose balances shall be light, are those who shall lose their souls, and shall remain in hell forever." One's good deeds must outweigh one's bad deeds.

Muslims generally believe one stands the best chance of salvation by mimicking the sayings and actions of Muhammad, the greatest of all humans. After all, Muhammad was pleasing to Allah, and if a Muslim can do and say what Muhammad said and did, perhaps he or she will end up in paradise. This is one reason Muslim tradition is so important, for it contains a record of what Muhammad did and said in various circumstances.

Many Muslims seem all too aware that they fall short of what might be expected of them on the day of judgment. They accordingly seek to engage in extra works so that, perhaps, they can tip the scales in their favor. Such individuals recite extra prayers, observe extra fasts, make more gifts to charity, repeat the 99 most beautiful names of Allah, go on pilgrimages (not just to Mecca but to other Muslim sites as well), and perform other good works—all in order to gain merit before Allah.

No Assurance

Even those who engage in all these extra good works have no guarantee or assurance of salvation. When a Muslim dies, he does not know whether he will go to paradise or to hell. As Ergun Mehmet Caner and Emir Fethi Caner put it, "Every Muslim fears the scales of justice, which weigh his good deeds against his bad deeds."[4] Judgment is based on the arbitrary will of Allah, and no one can predict what Allah's decision will be. "Fatalism is a belief that events are fixed in advance for all time in such a manner that human beings are powerless to change them. In this case, Allah will send to heaven whomever he pleases, and send to hell whomever he pleases."[5] Indeed, "one can be the most faithful of all believers in Allah and still rightly be sent to hell. Paradoxically, someone can be the worst person in the world and hypothetically still go to Paradise."[6] Even Muhammad himself was unsure about his salvation (Hadith 5:266)—and if he wasn't sure, how can any Muslim be sure?

The one exception to this is that anyone who dies in service to Allah—whether he is good or evil—is assured a place in paradise. This explains why radical Islamic terrorists are all too willing to give up their lives to attack infidels.

A CHRISTIAN RESPONSE

Original Sin

Contrary to the Muslim view, Adam and Eve's sin did not just affect them in a minimal way. In fact, Scripture teaches that Adam and Eve spiritually died the day they partook of the forbidden fruit.

The word *death* in the Bible carries the idea of separation. Physical death involves the separation of the soul or spirit from the body. Spiritual death involves the separation of the human being from God. When Adam and Eve partook of the forbidden fruit, they were immediately separated from God in a spiritual sense. The moment of their sin, they became "dead in…transgressions and sins" (Ephesians 2:1-3). Their spiritual separation from God eventually led to their physical deaths.

Also contrary to the Muslim view, Adam and Eve's sin did not affect them in an isolated way; it affected the entire human race. Ever since that fateful day, human beings enter the world at birth in a state of sin. The apostle Paul said "sin entered the world through one man, and death through sin, and in this way death came to all men, because all sinned" (Romans 5:12). He affirmed that "through the disobedience of the one man the many were made sinners" (Romans 5:19).

In keeping with this, David said in Psalm 51:5, "Surely I was sinful at birth, sinful from the time my mother conceived me" (see also Genesis 8:21; Psalm 53:3; Romans 3:10-11). According to this verse, human beings are born into the world in a state of sin. The sin nature is passed on from conception. This is why Ephesians 2:3 says we are "by nature objects of wrath."

The universality of sin bears witness to the reality of original sin. In Ecclesiastes 7:20 we read, "There is not a righteous man on earth who does what is right and never sins." In Isaiah 64:6 we read, "All of us have become like one who is unclean, and all our righteous acts are like filthy rags; we all shrivel up like a leaf, and like the wind our sins sweep us away." In Job 15:14-16 we read, "What is man, that he could be pure, or one born of woman, that he could be righteous? If God places no trust in his holy ones, if even the heavens are not pure in his eyes, how much less man, who is vile and corrupt, who drinks up evil like water!" In 1 John 1:8 we read, "If we claim to be without sin, we deceive ourselves and the truth is not in us." In view of these facts, we might say that a prime manifestation of this universal sin in the human heart is the Muslim denial of any sin problem at all.

A reasonable look at the empirical evidence in the world around us confirms man's depravity and fallenness instead of man's alleged innate goodness. John Ankerberg and John Weldon have observed that "since 3,600 B.C. the world has known only 292 years of peace. In that period, stretching more than 55 centuries, there have been an incredible 14,531 wars in which over 3.6 billion people have been killed."[7]

Though Muslims deny the doctrine of original sin, the Quran itself gives plenty of evidence that man has a sin problem:

- "The (human) soul is certainly prone to evil" (Sura 12:53).
- "Verily man was created anxious, fretful when evil touches him but mean-spirited when good reaches him" (Sura 70:19-21).
- "Man is given up to injustice and ingratitude" (Sura 14:34).
- "Man was created weak" (Sura 4:28).
- "(Man) becomes an open disputer" (Sura 16:4).
- "Man doth transgress all bounds" (Sura 96:6).
- "If God were to punish men for their wrongdoing, He would not leave, on the (earth), a single living creature" (Sura 16:61).

Sin—Not Feebleness or Forgetfulness

Contrary to the Muslim view that sin involves mere human feebleness and forgetfulness, Scripture indicates that sin involves active rebellion against a holy God and a violation of His holy law, and it shows that we are all guilty. A key meaning of *sin* in the Bible is "to miss the target." Sin is failure to live up to God's standards. All of us miss the target. Not one person is capable of fulfilling all of God's laws at all times.

The apostle Paul stressed that all human beings fall short of God's glory (Romans 3:23). The phrase *fall short* is a single word in the Greek, and it is in the present tense. This indicates continuing action. Human beings perpetually fall short of God's glory. The word *glory* here refers not just to God's splendor but to the outward manifestation of His attributes—including His righteousness, justice, and holiness. Human beings fall short of God in these and other areas.

Human sin always shows up clearly in the presence of God's

holiness. In the light of His holiness, the darkness of sin is undeniable. Remember what happened to the prophet Isaiah? He was a relatively righteous man. But when he beheld God in His infinite holiness, his own personal sin came into clear focus, and he could only say, "Woe to me!...I am ruined! For I am a man of unclean lips, and I live among a people of unclean lips" (Isaiah 6:5).

When we measure ourselves against other human beings, we may come out looking okay. In fact, to measure ourselves against other human beings might lead us to believe we are fairly righteous. But other human beings' behavior is not our moral measuring stick. God is. And as we measure ourselves against God in His infinite holiness and righteousness, our sin shows up in all its ugliness.

The seriousness of man's sin problem comes into clearest focus in the teachings of Jesus Christ. Jesus taught that man is capable of great wickedness (Mark 7:20-23). Moreover, He said that man is utterly lost (Luke 19:10), that he is a sinner (Luke 15:10), and that he is in need of repentance before a holy God (Mark 1:15).

Jesus often spoke of sin in metaphors that illustrate the havoc sin can wreak in one's life. He described sin as blindness (Matthew 23:16-26), sickness (Matthew 9:12), slavery (John 8:34), and darkness (John 8:12; 12:35-46). Moreover, Jesus taught that this is a universal condition and that all people are guilty before God (Luke 7:37-48).

Clearly, sin is not mere forgetfulness and feebleness. Consider the case of Adam. As noted previously, Muslims claim Adam made a mistake because he forgot God's command not to eat of the tree. This explanation stretches credulity; even the Quran says Satan reminded Adam of God's command as he was tempting Adam to eat of the fruit (Sura 7:20). Adam didn't forget. He actively chose rebellion!

Sin Is an Inner Reality

Jesus taught that both inner thoughts and external acts render a person guilty. For example, He asserted in Matthew 5:28 that "anyone who looks at a woman lustfully has already committed adultery with her in his heart." Likewise, He taught that from within the human heart come evil thoughts, sexual immorality, theft, murder, adultery, greed, malice, deceit, envy, slander, arrogance, and folly (Mark 7:21-23). Moreover, He affirmed that God is fully aware of every person's sins, both external acts and inner thoughts; nothing escapes His notice (Matthew 22:18; Luke 6:8; John 4:17-19). This means that at the future judgment of humanity, human beings will be required to give an account of not only their external deeds ("good deeds being weighed against bad deeds on a scale of justice"), but also what went on in their hearts as well.

To be sure, God will judge our external actions (Psalm 62:12; see also Matthew 16:27; Ephesians 6:7-8). But He will also judge that which goes on in our hearts and minds. The Lord "will bring to light what is hidden in darkness and will expose the motives of men's hearts" (1 Corinthians 4:5).

Good Works Not Enough

Contrary to the works-based salvation of Islam, God has revealed in the Bible that works do not save. The apostle Paul affirmed, "We maintain that a man is justified by faith apart from observing the law" (Romans 3:28). He said, "A man is not justified by observing the law, but by faith in Jesus Christ," for "by observing the law no one will be justified" (Galatians 2:16). "It is by grace you have been saved, through faith—and this not from yourselves, it is the gift of God—not by works, so that no one can boast" (Ephesians 2:8-9).

Paul, who wrote the above verses under the inspiration of the Holy Spirit, was formerly a Jew who sought to earn his relationship with God by observing the law, like any good Jew. He discovered what we must all discover—good works cannot bring us into God's favor, for even our best works fall far short of the magnificent holiness of God. "No one is good except God alone" (Mark 10:18). "All our righteous acts are like filthy rags" (Isaiah 64:6). Our best efforts fail!

This is not to say Christians give no place at all to good works in daily life, but these works play no role in salvation. Salvation comes about through faith (Romans 4:1-25; Galatians 3:6-14). Good works, however, are by-products of salvation (Matthew 7:15-23; 1 Timothy

5:10,25). Good works should result from the changed purpose for living that salvation brings (1 Corinthians 3).

Muslims must come to understand that Islam seeks to take forgetful and feeble men and make them better (by reminding them of Allah's law), but Christianity seeks to take dead men and make them spiritually alive (John 3:1-5,16-17). We are all born into this world spiritually dead (separated from God because of sin). By trusting in Christ, we are made spiritually alive. Islamic ethics won't cut it.

God's Declaration of Righteousness

The wonderful good news of salvation involves a theological word: *justification*. Justification is a singular and instantaneous event in which God declares the believing sinner to be righteous. *Justification* is a judicial term that refers to God's legal declaration. It is not based on performance or good works. It involves God's pardoning of sinners and declaring them absolutely righteous at the moment they trust in Christ for salvation (Romans 3:25,28,30; 8:33-34; Galatians 4:21–5:12; 1 John 1:7–2:2).

Here is the theological backdrop: Humankind's dilemma of falling short of God's glory (Romans 3:23) pointed to the need for a solution. Man's sin—his utter unrighteousness—prevented him from coming into a relationship with God on his own. Humankind was guilty before a holy God, and this guilt of sin put a barrier between man and God.

Justification is the solution. Negatively, this word means one is once-for-all pronounced not guilty before God. Positively, the word means one is once-for-all pronounced righteous before God. The very righteousness of Christ is imputed (credited or transferred) to the believer's life.

Note that this declaration is something external to man. It does not depend on man's personal level of righteousness or on anything man does. It depends solely on God's declaration. It is a once-for-all judicial pronouncement that takes place the moment a sinner believes in Christ. The person is yet a sinner and is experientially not righteous, but he is nevertheless righteous in God's sight because of justification.

Romans 3:24 tells us that God gives His declaration of righteousness to believers "freely by his grace." The word *grace* literally means "unmerited favor." God's unmerited favor allows Him to declare believers righteous. No one can earn this righteousness.

A key blessing that results from being declared righteous is that we now have peace with God (Romans 5:1). We might say that the Father sees believers through the lens of Jesus Christ. There is peace between the Father and Jesus Christ, so there is also peace between the Father and believers because believers are in Christ.

Necessity of an Atonement

God did not subjectively or arbitrarily decide to overlook man's sin or wink at his unrighteousness. Contrary to the Muslim denial of a need for an atonement, Scripture demonstrates that this atonement was absolutely necessary in order to make justification possible. Jesus died on the cross for us. He died in our stead. He paid for our sins. Jesus ransomed us from death by His own death on the cross (2 Corinthians 5:21).

Jesus Himself defines for us the nature of the atonement. He affirmed that He came into the world for the very purpose of dying (John 12:27). Moreover, He saw His death as a sacrificial offering for the sins of humanity (He said His blood "is poured out for many for the forgiveness of sins" in Matthew 26:26-28). He took His sacrificial mission with utmost seriousness, for He knew that without Him, humanity would certainly perish (Matthew 16:25; John 3:16) and spend eternity apart from God in a place of great suffering (Matthew 10:28; 11:23; 23:33; 25:41; Luke 16:22-28).

Jesus therefore described His mission this way: "The Son of Man did not come to be served, but to serve, and to give his life a ransom for many" (Matthew 20:28). "The Son of Man came to seek and to save what was lost" (Luke 19:10). "God did not send his Son into the world to condemn the world, but to save the world through him" (John 3:17).

In John 10, Jesus compares Himself to a good shepherd who not only gives His life to save the sheep (John 10:11) but also lays His life down of His own accord (John 10:18). This is precisely what Jesus did at the cross (Matthew 26:53-56): He laid His life down to atone for the sins of humanity.

This is certainly how others perceived His mission. When Jesus began His three-year ministry and was walking toward John the Baptist at the Jordan River, John said, "Look, the Lamb of God, who takes away the sin of the world!" (John 1:29). John's portrayal of Christ as the Lamb of God is a graphic affirmation that Jesus Himself would be the sacrifice that would atone for the sins of humanity (see Isaiah 53:7).

In Romans 3:25 we read, "God presented him as a sacrifice of atonement." The Greek word for "sacrifice of atonement" is rendered more literally *propitiation*. This word communicates the idea that Jesus' sacrificial death on the cross provided full satisfaction of God's holy demands against a sinful people, thereby averting His just wrath against them (Romans 1:18; 2:5,8; 3:5). Because of this propitiation, He can freely and justly declare us righteous and justified.

When you speak to a Muslim, I suggest you focus on Abraham's sacrifice of his son in the Old Testament (Genesis 22). In the Quran's depiction of this event, Abraham's son was ransomed from death by an animal sacrifice (Sura 37:102-107). These are the same words that describe what Jesus did at the cross (Matthew 20:28; 1 Corinthians 5:7; 1 Timothy 2:5-6; Hebrews 7:27; 9:15,28). The atoning sacrificial death of Christ is not un-Quranic. Abraham's story illustrates the need of a sacrifice to take another's place. Jesus as the Lamb of God took our place as a sacrifice so that we could be saved (John 1:29,36)!

Warning: Muslims believe Ishmael, not Isaac, was to be sacrificed by Abraham. I would simply avoid this issue and focus the major attention on sacrifice and ransom.[8] You can correct the minor error on Ishmael later.

The Certainty of Salvation

Contrary to the Muslim's lack of assurance of salvation, the Bible indicates that once a person becomes a part of the family of God by trusting in Christ, he or she is secure in salvation. Scripture affirms,

"Whom He predestined, He also called; and these whom He called, He also justified; and these whom He justified, He also glorified" (Romans 8:30 NASB). Here is an unbroken chain of events from pre-destination to glorification in heaven, and the past tense emphasizes the certainty of our final glorification. We are promised that "the gifts and the calling of God are irrevocable" (Romans 11:29). Scripture asserts, "God has given us eternal life, and this life is in His Son. He who has the Son has the life; he who does not have the Son of God does not have the life. These things I have written to you who believe in the name of the Son of God, *in order that you may know* that you have eternal life" (1 John 5:11-13, emphasis added).

Ephesians 4:30 indicates that believers are sealed for the day of redemption by the Holy Spirit (see also Ephesians 1:13). This seal—which indicates ownership, authority, and security—cannot be broken (even by the believer himself). The seal guarantees our entry into heaven.

Paul's metaphor would have been clear to first-century readers. Roman emperors sealed their letters with wax and then stamped them with their own personal seal. That seal would guarantee the letters would reach their final destinations. Anyone who opened the letters before they arrived would be put to death. The believer in Jesus is like a letter destined for heaven, and the Holy Spirit (God Himself) is our seal, guaranteeing that we will reach our final destination.

Besides this, the Father keeps us in His sovereign hands, and no one can take us out of His hands (John 10:28-30; 13:1). God has us in His firm grip, and He will never let us go.

Not only that, but the Lord Jesus Himself regularly intercedes and prays for us (Hebrews 7:25). His work of intercession, as our divine High Priest, is necessary because of our weaknesses, our helplessness, and our immaturity as children of God. He knows our limitations, and He knows the power and the strategy of the foe with whom we have to contend (Satan). He is therefore faithful in making intercession for us, and His prayers are always answered.

Muslims desperately need to hear of this glorious salvation in Jesus Christ!

7

JUDGMENT DAY, HEAVEN, AND HELL

THE QURAN SPEAKS ABOUT DEATH, resurrection, the future day of judgment, heaven, and hell. It may not tell us as much as we would like to know on these subjects, but its pages provide enough data for us to construct a picture of the Muslim expectation of the afterlife.

The Quran recognizes that every human being dies. We read, "Every soul shall have a taste of death" (Sura 3:185). Indeed, at death "the angels stretch forth their hands (saying), 'Yield up your souls'" (Sura 6:93). Following death, the Muslim faces a future day of resurrection and judgment, and with no assurance of salvation among Muslims, this can be a frightening prospect. The death of unbelievers is especially frightful: "If thou couldst see, when the angels take the souls of the Unbelievers (at death), (How) they smite their faces and their backs, (saying): 'Taste the penalty of the blazing Fire'" (Sura 8:50).

As we noted previously, one group of Muslims is guaranteed direct entrance into paradise (heaven): martyrs who die in the service of Allah. All other believers must await the future day of resurrection. Between death and resurrection, people are in a very deep sleep. People will not know until they awaken on the day of resurrection whether they are to go to hell or to paradise.[1]

THE MUSLIM VIEW OF THE AFTERLIFE

Resurrection and Judgment

Muslims believe Allah will one day resurrect all who have died. The day and the hour are not known to mortals. At the last day, Allah will sound a trumpet, the earth will be split, and the bodies of human beings will rejoin their souls. Allah will re-create each individual's body and rejoin his or her soul to it. In the Quran we read, "See they not that God, who created the heavens and the earth…is able to give life to the dead? Yea, clearly he has the power over all things" (Sura 46:33). Many Muslims believe this to be a physical resurrection; others believe in a spiritual resurrection.

Following the resurrection, human beings will be judged. They will be face-to-face with Allah and will have to give an account for all their actions. The Quran teaches that "only on the day of judgment shall you be paid your full recompense" (Sura 3:185).

Allah will judge people on the scale of absolute justice. The scale is used to weigh one's good and bad deeds. Good deeds will be placed in one pan of the balance, and evil deeds in the other. If the good deeds are heavy enough to tip the scale, the person will go to paradise (subject to Allah's arbitrary decision). If, however, one's evil deeds are heavier, he will be cast into the fires of hell. The Quran affirms, "Then those whose balance (of good deeds) is heavy, they will attain salvation: But those whose balance is light, will be those who have lost their souls, in Hell will they abide" (Sura 23:102-103). This essentially means that one must be at least 51 percent good to get into paradise.[2] This judgment will be based on the records of two recording angels who keep track of good and bad deeds throughout one's life.

One Muslim writer describes the route to one's eternal destiny this way: "When the trial of judgment is over those destined to Hell or Paradise will be made to pass over a narrow bridge to their respective destinations. The bridge is so fashioned that the favored will cross with ease and facility while the condemned will tumble off into Hell."[3]

Heaven

The Muslim whose good deeds outweigh his bad deeds can

look forward to a place of unimaginable delight. The Quran teaches that Muslims in paradise enjoy lofty mansions (39:20), thrones (18:31), rivers, and fantastic food (52:17-24). They also experience joy (36:55-58), peace (19:61-63), satisfaction (43:68-73), and bliss (69:21-24).[4]

The Quran pictures heaven as a beautiful green garden of bliss with flowing water and shade. Believers receive whatever their hearts desire. Faithful men are even promised the companionship of young and beautiful women. The faithful will lie on soft silken couches and "will enjoy gentle speech, pleasant shade, and every available fruit, as well as all the cool drink and meat they desire. They will drink from a shining stream of delicious wine, from which they will suffer no intoxicating aftereffects" (Sura 37:45-47).

Apparently the Muslim heaven is massive. We read of a tree in paradise so big that a rider can travel in its shade for a hundred years without passing out of it.[5] Muslims can take leisurely walks anywhere in paradise, and on all sides the view is spectacular and includes fountains, pavilions, and rivers.[6]

Hell

Hell is for those whose evil deeds outweigh their good deeds on the scale of absolute justice. Muslims view hell as a place of unimaginable suffering. It is a place of scalding winds and black smoke.[7] The Quran teaches that there will be "a fierce blast of fire and boiling water, and in the shades of black smoke" (Sura 56:42-43). The boiling water melts the skin, which is immediately replaced with new skin so the person can taste the torment of hell anew. Brains boil, and molten lead is poured into the ears.[8]

The Quran says, "When they are cast, bound together, into a constricted place therein, they will plead for destruction there and then" (Sura 25:13). The person suffering such a destiny can neither escape nor perish.[9] The horror of evil is reflected in the fact that people there neither live nor die but simply suffer in fire (Sura 87:12-13). So consistent is the suffering that people become intensely weary from trying to escape the fires of hell (Sura 88:3-4). Some Muslims interpret the horrible descriptions of hell spiritually, but the majority takes them quite literally.[10]

Even the food in hell is bad. The Quran teaches, "No food for them save bitter thorn-fruit which doth not nourish nor release from hunger" (Sura 88:6-7). This is in noted contrast to the wonderful foods and wine of paradise.

Interestingly, Muslim tradition tells us that the majority of occupants in hell are women. "I stood at the gate of the Fire and found that the majority of the people entering it were women" (Hadith 8:555).

Some Muslims view hell as a kind of Islamic purgatory. They believe Muslims will have to spend time in hell to pay for their sins before being granted the privilege of entering paradise (Hadith 8:577). The amount of time each respective Muslim must stay in hell depends on the gravity and degree of his sin. Religious hypocrites—people who claimed to be Muslim but were not—will remain in hell forever.[11] Phil Parshall reports that "hypocrisy carries with it an extreme penalty. With intestines protruding outward, the sinner is made to go around hell confessing to people that he held to a double standard in life."[12]

Some Muslim traditions allude to hearing the voices of dead people in cemeteries. The dead cry out in torment as a result of their suffering in hell. In one tradition, we read that a person is being punished in hell because he neglected to engage in ritual cleansing following urination. Muhammad categorized this as a major sin.[13] This reflects the strict legalism of Islam.

THE CHRISTIAN VIEW OF THE AFTERLIFE

Judgment

The Muslim and Christian views of the afterlife do share some similarities, but the differences are notable. One key difference is that Muslims believe the purpose of the judgment is to determine whether or not a person is worthy of salvation, and following that determination, the person is sent to either heaven or hell. The Christian view is that a person's destiny is settled before the judgment, for God knows who has and who has not trusted in Christ. Scripture indicates that the spirits of believers go straight to heaven at death (2 Corinthians 5:8), and the spirits of nonbelievers go to a place of suffering (Luke 16:19-31). Both await the future resurrection. Further, the Bible describes two judgments that will take place in the future—the judgment of believers at the Judgment Seat of Christ, and the judgment of nonbelievers at the Great White Throne judgment.

Another distinction relates to the God one will face at the judgment. In the Christian view, people will face a God whose attributes are absolutely consistent. That is to say, the Christian God is consistently holy (Leviticus 19:2). He is always pure in every way and is separate from all that is morally imperfect. He is also singularly good, just, and righteous (Habakkuk 1:13; Matthew 5:48; 1 John 1:5). The God of the Bible abhors evil, does not create evil, and does not lead men astray.

In contrast, the Muslim must face Allah, who sometimes does good and other times evil, who sometimes shows mercy and other times cruelty. Allah need not adhere to an absolute standard of righteousness. As John Elder explains, "*Right* is what Allah commands at a given time; *wrong* is that which He forbids at a given time. And what He commands at one time, He may forbid at another."[14] For example, Muhammad recorded certain revelations in the Quran from Allah that were considered final truth, only to have those revelations abrogated by other revelations from Allah later on.

The prospect of appearing before such an arbitrary God creates a sense of profound uncertainty and insecurity. Indeed, as Elder notes, "if Allah is not bound to consistently act righteously, there can be no certainty as to what He may decide to do on the Judgment Day. Allah's sovereignty allows Him to make decisions that may seem inconsistent and arbitrary in man's view."[15]

The Judgment of Christians. All believers will one day stand before the Judgment Seat of Christ (Romans 14:8-10; 1 Corinthians 3:11-15). At that time Christ will examine each believer's deeds. Personal motives and intents of the heart will also be weighed.

This judgment has nothing to do with whether or not the Christian will remain saved. Those who have placed faith in Christ are saved, and nothing threatens that. Believers are eternally secure in their salvation (Romans 8:30; Ephesians 4:30). This judgment rather has to do with the reception or loss of rewards.

Scripture indicates that some believers at the judgment may have a sense of deprivation and suffer some degree of forfeiture and shame. Indeed, they may forfeit certain rewards that they otherwise might have received, and this will involve a sense of loss. The fact is, Christians differ radically in holiness of conduct and faithfulness in service. God in His justice and holiness takes all this into account. For this reason, 2 John 8 warns us, "Watch out that you do not lose what you have worked for, but that you may be rewarded fully." In 1 John 2:28 John wrote about the possibility of a believer actually being ashamed at Christ's coming.

We must keep all this in perspective, however. The prospect of living eternally with Christ in heaven is something that should give each of us joy. And our joy will last for all eternity.

The scope of the judgment includes actions. Numerous Scripture verses reveal that the Lord will judge each of our actions. The psalmist said to the Lord, "Surely you will reward each person according to what he has done" (Psalm 62:12; see Matthew 16:27). In Ephesians 6:7-8 we read that the Lord "will reward everyone for whatever good he does, whether he is slave or free."

The scope of the judgment includes thoughts. At the Judgment Seat of Christ, our thoughts will also be scrutinized. In Jeremiah 17:10 God said, "I the LORD search the heart and examine the mind, to reward a man according to his conduct, according to what his deeds deserve." The Lord "will bring to light what is hidden in darkness and will expose the motives of men's hearts" (1 Corinthians 4:5). The Lord is the One "who searches hearts and minds" (Revelation 2:23).

The scope of the judgment includes words. Christ once said that "men will have to give account on the day of judgment for every careless word they have spoken" (Matthew 12:36). This is an important aspect of judgment, for tremendous damage can be done through the human tongue (see James 3:1-12).

Rewards and crowns. What kinds of rewards will believers receive at the Judgment Seat of Christ? Scripture often speaks of them in terms of crowns that we wear. It mentions several different crowns that symbolize various achievements and awards in the Christian life.

The crown of life is given to those who persevere under trial, and especially to those who suffer to the point of death (James 1:12; Revelation 2:10). The crown of glory is given to those who faithfully and sacrificially minister God's Word to the flock (1 Peter 5:4). The crown incorruptible is given to those who win the race of temperance and self-control (1 Corinthians 9:25). The crown of righteousness is given to those who long for the second coming of Christ (2 Timothy 4:8).

The Judgment of Nonbelievers. Unlike believers, whose judgment deals only with rewards and loss of rewards, nonbelievers face a horrific judgment that leads to their being cast into the lake of fire. The judgment that nonbelievers face is called the Great White Throne judgment (Revelation 20:11-15). Christ is the divine Judge, and those He judges are the unsaved dead of all time. The judgment takes place at the end of the millennial kingdom, Christ's 1000-year reign on the earth.

Those who face Christ at this judgment will be judged on the basis of their works (Revelation 20:12-13). It is critical to understand that they actually get to this judgment because they are already unsaved. This judgment will not separate believers from unbelievers, for all who will experience it will have already made the choice during their lifetimes to reject salvation in Jesus Christ. Once they are before the divine Judge, they are judged according to their works not only to justify their condemnation but to determine the degree to which each person should be punished throughout eternity.

Resurrected to judgment. Those who participate in the Great White Throne judgment are resurrected to judgment. Jesus Himself affirmed that "a time is coming when all who are in their graves will hear his voice and come out—those who have done good will rise to live, and those who have done evil will rise to be condemned" (John 5:28-29).

We need to emphasize, though, that Jesus is not teaching that there is just one general resurrection that will take place at the end of time. Contrary to this idea, the Scriptures indicate that there are two types of resurrection, referred to as the "first resurrection" and the "second resurrection" (Revelation 20:5-6,11-15). The first resurrection is the resurrection of Christians; the second resurrection is the resurrection of the wicked.

The second resurrection is an awful spectacle. All the unsaved of all time will be resurrected at the end of Christ's millennial kingdom, judged at the Great White Throne judgment, and then cast alive into the lake of fire (Revelation 20:11-15). Unsaved human beings will be given bodies that will last forever, which means they will be subject to pain and suffering forever.

Degrees of punishment. The Scriptures indicate that all those who are judged at the Great White Throne judgment have a horrible destiny ahead. Indeed, their destiny generally will involve weeping and gnashing of teeth (Matthew 13:41-42), condemnation (Matthew 12:36-37), destruction (Philippians 1:28), eternal punishment (Matthew 25:46), separation from God's presence (2 Thessalonians 1:8-9), and trouble and distress (Romans 2:9). Nevertheless, the Scriptures also note degrees of punishment in hell. These degrees of punishment will be determined at the Great White Throne judgment, when Christ examines each person with His penetrating eyes (see Matthew 10:15; 16:27; Luke 12:47-48; Revelation 20:12-13; 22:12).

In view of these facts, we find three major faults with the Muslim view of judgment:

1. The purpose of the judgment is not to determine whether one is saved.
2. The righteous and the wicked do not experience the same judgment.
3. God is not arbitrary; He judges with an absolute standard of righteousness.

Heaven

Christians disagree with the Muslim view that heaven is a sensual place of pleasure, where faithful men can have 72 beautiful maidens at their disposal and eat, drink, and enjoy full bodily satisfaction.

Such a view goes against the entire tenor of Scripture, in which God reveals that His standard for the human race is and always has been monogamy (Genesis 1:27; 2:21-25; Deuteronomy 17:17; Matthew 19:4; 1 Corinthians 7:2; 1 Timothy 3:2,12).

Besides, sexual conjugation is not even an issue in heaven, for Jesus taught, "At the resurrection people will neither marry nor be given in marriage; they will be like the angels in heaven" (Matthew 22:30). The context here indicates that once believers receive their glorified resurrection bodies, the need for procreation (one of the fundamental purposes for marriage) will no longer exist. We will be like the angels in the sense that we will not be married and will not procreate any longer. The idea that the faithful will have sex in heaven for pure pleasure does not come from Scripture.

A full biblical description of heaven and the many blessings that accompany life there is beyond the scope of this chapter. But a look at just a few key aspects of heaven is enough to show that it is not designed to provide sensual pleasure.

Paradise. I purposefully begin my discussion with the fact that the Christian Bible sometimes uses the word *paradise* to describe heaven, though it does not mean what Muslims mean by the term. The word *paradise* literally means "garden of pleasure" or "garden of delight." Revelation 2:7 makes reference to heaven as the "paradise of God." The apostle Paul said he "was caught up to paradise" and "heard inexpressible things, things that man is not permitted to tell" (2 Corinthians 12:4). Yet nowhere are we told that this "garden of delight" is a place where sensual pleasure abounds with 72 beautiful maidens at the disposal of men. The primary reasons heaven will be so delightful are that God Himself is there, Satan will be barred, and there will be no sin. Life will be perfect! Who can deny that one reason for the pleasures of heaven is direct access to God? Psalm 16:11 says, "You will fill me with joy in your presence, with eternal pleasures at your right hand."

A holy city. Revelation 21:1-2 describes heaven as "the holy city." This is a fitting description, for this city will have no sin or unrighteousness (including unbridled sensuality) of any kind. Only the pure of heart will dwell there. This does not mean you and I must personally attain moral perfection in order to dwell there. Those of us who believe in Christ have been given the very righteousness of Christ. Because of what Christ accomplished for us at the cross (taking our sins upon Himself), we have been made holy (Hebrews 10:14). Therefore, we will have the privilege of living for all eternity in the holy city.

The home of righteousness. Second Peter 3:13 tells us that "in keeping with his promise we are looking forward to a new heaven and a new earth, the home of righteousness." What a perfect environment this will be to live in. During our earthly lives, we have to lock up our houses, and we fear the possibility of intruders breaking in. Unrighteousness is all around us. But heaven will be the home of righteousness. It will therefore be a perfect living environment for those who have been made righteous by Christ.

The absence of death. The Old Testament promises that in the heavenly state, death will be swallowed up forever (Isaiah 25:8). Paul speaks of this same reality as it relates to the future resurrection: "When the perishable has been clothed with the imperishable, and the mortal with immortality, then the saying that is written will come true: 'Death has been swallowed up in victory'" (1 Corinthians 15:54). Revelation 21:4 tells us that God "will wipe every tear from their eyes. There will be no more death or mourning or crying or pain, for the old order of things has passed away." Death will be gone and done with, never again to plague those who dwell in heaven. Life in the eternal city will be painless, tearless, and deathless.

Intimate fellowship with God and Christ. Can anything be more sublime and more utterly satisfying for the Christian than to enjoy the sheer delight of unbroken fellowship with God and to have immediate and completely unobstructed access to the divine glory (John 14:3; 2 Corinthians 5:6-8; Philippians 1:23; 1 Thessalonians 4:17)? We shall see him "face to face" in all His splendor and glory. We will gaze upon His countenance and behold His resplendent beauty forever.

Surely our greatest joy and most exhilarating thrill will be to look upon the face of the divine Creator and fellowship with Him forever. He "who alone is immortal and who lives in unapproachable light"

(1 Timothy 6:16) shall reside intimately among His own, and "they will be his people, and God himself will be among them" (Revelation 21:3).

In the afterlife, our fellowship with the Lord will no longer be intermittent, blighted by sin and defeat. Instead, we will enjoy continuous fellowship. Spiritual death shall never again cause human beings to lose fellowship with God because believers' sin problem will no longer exist.

Reunion with Christian loved ones. One of the most glorious aspects of our lives in heaven is that we will be reunited with Christian loved ones (see 1 Thessalonians 4:13-17). This is something to truly look forward to.

Satisfaction of all needs. In our present life on earth, we often go hungry and thirsty. Our needs are not always met. But in the eternal state, God will abundantly meet each and every need. As we read in Revelation 7:16-17, "Never again will they hunger; never again will they thirst. The sun will not beat upon them, nor any scorching heat. For the Lamb at the center of the throne will be their shepherd; he will lead them to springs of living water. And God will wipe away every tear from their eyes."

Serene rest. The Scriptures indicate that a key feature of heavenly life is rest (Revelation 14:13). No more deadlines to work toward. No more overtime work in order to make ends meet. No more breaking one's back. Just rest. Sweet serene rest. And our rest will be especially sweet since it is in the very presence of God, who meets our every need.

Hell

Hell is as awful as heaven is wonderful. The Scriptures assure us that hell is a real place. But hell was not part of God's original creation, which He called "good" (Genesis 1). Hell was created later to accommodate the banishment of Satan and his fallen angels who rebelled against God (Matthew 25:41). Human beings who reject Christ will join Satan and his fallen angels in this infernal place of suffering.

The Scriptures employ a variety of descriptions of the horrors of hell, including fire, fiery furnace, unquenchable fire, the lake of burning sulfur, the lake of fire, everlasting contempt, perdition, the place of weeping and gnashing of teeth, eternal punishment, darkness, the wrath to come, exclusion, torments, damnation, condemnation, retribution, woe, and the second death. Hell is a horrible destiny (see Matthew 13:42; 18:8; 25:41; Jude 7; Revelation 14:10; 19:20; 20:10).

Christians take exception to the Muslim view that people keep getting new skin so they can suffer the horrors of hell anew. Scripture is clear that unbelievers receive a permanent resurrection body just as believers do, but they will spend eternity in their resurrection bodies suffering in hell (see John 5:28-29; Revelation 20:5-6,11-15). No new skin will be necessary.

Unquestionably the greatest pain suffered by those in hell is not physical pain but their permanent exclusion from the presence of God. If ecstatic joy is found in the presence of God (Psalm 16:11), profound heartache and disillusionment are found in the absence of His presence.

Conclusion

How heartbreaking to know that Muslims die every day, hoping that Allah might have mercy on them and bring them to paradise. The reality is that to believe in Allah is to believe in a false god. To believe that submission to Allah brings salvation is to believe in a false gospel.

If we Christians really believe heaven is as wonderful as the Bible describes it, then shouldn't that be motivation enough for each of us to share this wonderful good news with our Muslim acquaintances?

HAS THE BIBLE
BEEN CORRUPTED?

MUSLIMS FACE A DILEMMA when dealing with the Christian Bible. According to the Quran, believers in Allah are not to reject any of Allah's Scriptures. If they obey the Quran, they are forbidden from accepting only a part of Allah's revelation to humankind (revelation that includes the Bible) (see Sura 4:136). Muslims are even commanded to consult the Hebrew and Greek Scriptures for confirmation of Muhammad's revelations (Sura 10:94). However, if they accept what the Bible teaches—that Jesus is the Son of God, Jesus in the Incarnation was God in human flesh, God is a Trinity, salvation is by faith in Christ, and so forth—then they must reject what the Quran teaches. In that case, they would no longer be Muslims. How then can Muslims solve this dilemma?

THE MUSLIM VIEW OF THE BIBLE

Muslims claim the original Bible was the Word of God (apparently still in good shape during the time of Muhammad—see Suras 2:136; 3:3; 5:48; 29:46), but then Jews and Christians corrupted it.[1] The Bible of today has been mingled with many "untruths" and contradictions. These untruths relate particularly to areas where the Bible disagrees with the Quran.

Muslim apologist Ajijola thus makes this assertion:

> The first five books of the Old Testament do not constitute the original Torah, but parts of the Torah have been mingled up with other narratives written by human beings and the original guidance of the Lord is lost in that quagmire. Similarly the four Gospels of Christ are not the original Gospels as they came from the prophet Jesus…The original and the fictitious, the divine and human are so intermingled that the grain cannot be separated from the chaff. The fact is that the original Word of God is preserved neither with the Jews nor with the Christians.[2]

Muslims believe, then, that what used to be the Word of God in the Bible has been so adulterated by human hands that it is now hardly distinguishable from the word of man (see Sura 3:71,78). Some verses may retain a glimmer of the truth Jesus taught, but these are few and far between in "the jungles of interpolations and contradictions with which the Bible is dense."[3]

Muslims say the Jews inserted many things into the Old Testament that served to personally benefit them. Muslim apologist Maurice Bucaille, for example, claims that "a revelation is mingled in all these writings, but all we possess today is what men have seen fit to leave us. These men manipulated the texts to please themselves, according to the circumstances they were in and the necessities they had to meet."[4]

This is illustrated in the Muslim claim that Muslims are the rightful heirs to the promises made to Abraham through Ishmael (his firstborn son), but the Jews, for personal gain, concocted a story (and inserted it into the Old Testament) to the effect that Isaac became Abraham's heir, and the inheritance from Abraham includes possession of the land of Palestine. In this Jewish version, Ishmael and his descendants became outcasts.[5] The original Old Testament, we are told, did not have this concocted story.

In the New Testament, Muslims claim Christians inserted the doctrine of Jesus being the Son of God, the doctrine of the Trinity, and other beliefs. The original New Testament did not contain such ideas, we are told. The original Jesus presented Himself as a mere prophet of Allah. Christians then took it upon themselves to deify this prophet. Today's New Testament, then, does not contain the actual words of Jesus but rather words that were put into His mouth by Christians. Today's New Testament is corrupt.

Some Muslims claim Jesus' original gospel was lost by the early church, and certain men—including Matthew, Mark, Luke, and John—set out to reconstruct the written life of Christ. But these accounts all contradict each other and are entirely unreliable. Muslims do not want man-made versions of the gospel, written by men; they want the original gospel handed down to the prophet Jesus.[6] (These Muslims do not explain how their negative view of Matthew, Mark, Luke, and John relates to the fact that Muhammad commended the reading of the entire Bible of his day [Sura 10:94].)

Amazingly, Muslim apologist Ahmed Deedat has argued that "out of over four thousand differing manuscripts the Christians boast about, the church fathers just selected four which tallied with their prejudices and called them Gospels of Matthew, Mark, Luke and John."[7] Further, Muslim apologists argue that none of the New Testament Gospel writers were eyewitnesses to what happened. Bucaille writes: "We do not in fact have an eyewitness account from the life of Jesus, contrary to what many Christians imagine."[8]

Muslims also claim innumerable variants (mistakes) exist among the various manuscript copies of the Bible. For example, one Muslim writer says "it is admitted by the most learned men in the Hebrew language, that the present English version of the Old Testament contains at least 100,000 errors (this would amount to approximately three errors in every verse)."[9]

Additionally, we are told that there is only one version of the Quran, whereas many different translations of the Bible are available today (NASB, NIV, KJV, and so forth). Muslims thus charge that we can trust the Quran, but we surely cannot trust the Bible.

Many modern Muslim apologists have concluded from these issues that the Bible is merely a human book—"the handiwork of man."[10] One must wonder whether they realize they're contradicting Muhammad when they argue so stringently against the Bible.

A CHRISTIAN RESPONSE

The authenticity and reliability of the Bible is one of the most important foundational facts to establish when dialoguing with Muslims. In responding to Muslim claims about the Bible, we must answer their objections and criticisms of the Bible as well as provide a positive statement of its trustworthiness.

Require Proof the Bible Has Been Changed

Claiming the Bible has been corrupted is one thing. Proving that claim is another thing entirely. One of the first things to do when a Muslim tells you the Bible has been corrupted is to ask for indisputable historical proof.

Demonstrate the Impossibility of Such a Change

To suppose the Bible became corrupted during or after Muhammad's time is entirely unreasonable. We can share these relevant factors with Muslims:

- Hundreds of thousands of copies of the Bible were dispersed over a large part of the world by Muhammad's time. Successfully corrupting the Bible would require changing nearly all those copies.

- Hundreds of years before Muhammad was even born, the Bible had already been translated into several languages. Would Muslims have us believe these various translations were identically altered all over the world so they would have a uniform corruption?

- Muslims claim that both Jews and Christians were involved in corrupting the Bible. But Jews and Christians of that time were hostile to one another, and if either party tried to alter the biblical text, the other party would have exposed the attempt.[11] Further, many dissenting Christian sects existed at this time. An alteration of the biblical text by any one of these sects would have brought immediate condemnation by the others.

- If the Jews had corrupted their Scriptures, wouldn't they have at least changed all the horrible things we read about them in the Torah, such as their total unfaithfulness during the wilderness sojourn and their participation in idolatry?[12] Likewise, if Christians corrupted the New Testament, wouldn't they have removed unflattering episodes about Christians, such as Peter denying Christ three times and the disciples scattering like a bunch of faithless cowards when Christ was arrested?

- Would the almighty and sovereign God of the universe allow His Word to become corrupted like this?

The Quran Indicates God's Word Cannot Be Changed

Sura 2:75 refers to the Bible as "the word of God." Sura 6:115 adds, "None can change His [Allah's] words." "There is no changing the Words of Allah" (Sura 10:64). If the Bible is God's Word, as the Quran says, and if God's Word cannot be changed, how can Muslims charge that the Bible has been corrupted without disagreeing with the Quran? Muslims claim the Bible contains contradictions, but they need to explain their own contradiction in saying the Bible has been changed when the Quran says God's Word cannot be changed.[13]

The Bible Argues Against the Possibility of Corruption

The charge that the Bible has been corrupted not only goes against what the Quran says, it also contradicts what the Bible itself teaches. In Isaiah 40:8 we read, "The grass withers and the flowers fall, but the word of our God stands forever." Likewise, in the New Testament, Jesus says, "Heaven and earth will pass away, but my words will never pass away" (Matthew 24:35).

The almighty God who had the power and sovereign control to inspire the Scriptures in the first place is surely going to continue to exercise His power and sovereign control in the preservation of Scripture. Further, the very text of the Bible illustrates God's ability to preserve Scripture. By examining how Christ viewed the Old Testament (keeping in mind that Jesus did not have in His possession the original books penned by the Old Testament writers, but possessed only copies), we see that He had full confidence that the Scriptures He used had been faithfully preserved through the centuries.

> Because Christ raised no doubts about the adequacy of the Scripture as His contemporaries knew them, we can safely assume that the first-century text of the Old Testament was a wholly adequate representation of the divine word originally given. Jesus regarded the extant copies of His day as so approximate to the originals in their message that He appealed to those copies as authoritative.[14]

The respect Jesus and His apostles held for the extant Old Testament text is an expression of their confidence that God providentially preserved these copies and translations so that they were substantially identical with the inspired originals. We can deduce that the same is true regarding the New Testament and God's preservation of the entire Bible through history.

An Inconsistent View of the Bible

Even though Muslims go to great lengths to argue for the corruption of the biblical text, they immediately accept the authenticity of any biblical text they feel lends support to their viewpoint. For example, Muslims argue from Deuteronomy 18 that Muhammad is the fulfillment of the prediction of a "great prophet" to come. Muslims argue from John 14 that Muhammad is "the comforter" of which Jesus spoke. Should Muslims accept Bible verses they think lend support to Islam while rejecting all the verses that do not?

Manuscript Evidence

Muhammad clearly commended the reading of the Bible of his day (Suras 5:69; 10:94). Abundant manuscript evidence proves today's Bible is the same Bible that existed during (and before) Muhammad's day. Indeed, more than 5000 partial and complete manuscript copies of the New Testament exist.

- The Chester Beatty papyrus (P45) dates to the third century AD, and contains the four Gospels and the Book of Acts (chapters 4–17). (P = papyrus.)

- The Chester Beatty papyrus (P46) dates to about AD 200 and contains ten Pauline epistles (all but the pastorals) and the Book of Hebrews.

- The Chester Beatty papyrus (P47) dates to the third century AD, and contains Revelation 9:10–17:2.

- The Bodmer Papyrus (P66) dates to about AD 200 and contains the Gospel of John.

- The Bodmer Papyrus (P75) dates to the early third century and contains Luke and John.

- The Sinaiticus uncial manuscript dates to the fourth century and contains the entire New Testament.

- The Vaticanus uncial manuscript dates to the fourth century and contains most of the New Testament except part of Hebrews, the pastoral epistles, Philemon, and Revelation.[15]

This means that massive manuscript evidence for the New Testament existed before Muhammad was even born. Our Bible translations today are based on these early manuscripts, so the Muslim charge of corruption since Muhammad's time is obliterated.

We also have some 86,000 quotations of the New Testament from the early church fathers and several thousand lectionaries (church-service books containing Scripture quotations used in the early centuries of Christianity). In fact, if we did not have a single manuscript copy of the Bible, scholars could still reconstruct all but 11 verses of the entire New Testament from quotations from the early church fathers written within 150 to 200 years from the time of Christ.[16]

What About the Variants?

In the thousands of manuscript copies we possess of the New Testament, scholars have discovered some 200,000 variants. This may seem like a staggering figure to the uninformed mind, but to people who study the issue, the numbers of variants are not so damning as they may initially appear.

More than 99 percent of these variants hold virtually no significance whatsoever. Many of these simply involve a missing letter in a word; some involve reversing the order of two words (such as "Christ Jesus" instead of "Jesus Christ"). Some may involve the absence of one or more insignificant words. Only about 40 of the variants have any real significance, and they do not affect any doctrine of the Christian faith or moral commandment. In more than 99 percent of the cases, the original text can be reconstructed to a practical certainty.

The science of textual criticism—comparing all the available manuscripts with each other—helps us come to an assurance regarding what the original document likely said. An illustration might be helpful.

Let us suppose we have five manuscript copies of an original document that no longer exists. Each of the manuscript copies is different. Our goal is to compare the manuscript copies and ascertain what the original must have said. Here are the five copies:

Manuscript #1: Jesus Christ is the Savior of the whole world.

Manuscript #2: Christ Jesus is the Savior of the whole world.

Manuscript #3: Jesus Christ the Savior of the whole worl.

Manuscript #4: Jesus is Savior of the whle world.

Manuscript #5: Jesus Christ is the Savor of the wrld.

Could you compare the manuscript copies and ascertain what the original document said with a high degree of certainty that you are correct? Of course you could.

This illustration is extremely simplistic, but a great majority of the 200,000 variants are solved by this method. By comparing the various manuscripts, most of which contain relatively minor differences like those above, the original content becomes fairly clear. Further, the sheer volume of manuscripts we possess greatly narrows the margin of doubt regarding what the original biblical document said.

Bible scholar Winfried Corduan has pointed out that if someone in the past had burned all the textual variants of the Bible, just as Caliph Uthman burned all the Quran variants, we would have a single manuscript of the Bible, just as Muslims have an "authoritative manuscript" of the Quran. Corduan notes that "the very existence of so many variant readings allows us to recover what the original must have said with a great degree of confidence. By contrast, it is impossible to restore the Quran to what existed prior to Uthman, since we now have only one version of the Quran—the one Uthman wanted us to have."[17]

Because Muslims often attack the Old Testament as being untrustworthy, I want to mention the Dead Sea Scrolls in this regard. In these scrolls, discovered at Qumran in 1947, we have Old Testament manuscripts that date about a thousand years earlier (150 BC) than the other Old Testament manuscripts previously in our possession (which dated to AD 980). The two sets of manuscripts are essentially the same with very few changes. The fact that manuscripts separated by a thousand years are essentially the same indicates the incredible accuracy of the Old Testament's manuscript transmission.

The copy of the Book of Isaiah discovered at Qumran illustrates this accuracy. Dr. Gleason Archer, who personally examined both the AD 980 and 150 BC copies of Isaiah, made this comment:

> Even though the two copies of Isaiah discovered in Qumran Cave 1 near the Dead Sea in 1947 were a thousand years earlier than the oldest dated manuscript previously known (AD 980), they proved to be word for word identical with our standard Hebrew Bible in more than 95 percent of the text. The 5 percent of variation consisted chiefly of obvious slips of the pen and variations in spelling.[18]

This means that Muslim apologists like Ahmed Deedat and Maurice Bucaille, in their attempt to prove corruptions in the Bible, are arguing against the same Bible that existed in the time of Muhammad and which Muhammad and the Quran indicated was trustworthy. Would Deedat and Bucaille say Muhammad was wrong? Would they say the Quran was in error?

Muhammad Did Not Understand the Bible

Two pivotal and undeniable facts are before us:

First, the Quran teaches there is one God named Allah. He is not a Trinity and cannot have a son because this would associate partners with God. Jesus was merely a prophet, not God, and not the Son of God. He did not die for man's sins. Salvation is attained through submission and obedience to Allah.

Second, the Bible teaches that God's name is Yahweh, and He is a Trinity. The second person of the Godhead is Jesus, and He is known by the ascription, "Son of God." Jesus is eternal God, and in the Incarnation He was God in human flesh. Salvation is attained by placing personal faith in Jesus, who died on the cross for man's sins.

In view of such contradictory doctrinal statements, what are we to make of Muhammad's commending of the Bible of his day (Suras 5:69; 10:94)? We know the Bible of his day is the same as the Bible of our day, so only one conclusion is possible: Muhammad really did not understand the essential teachings of Christianity, or he wouldn't have commended the Bible. Earlier in the book, I presented evidence that the versions of Christianity Muhammad was exposed to came from Nestorians and Ebionites, and both groups followed heretical perversions of Christianity. The prophet of the Quran was ignorant regarding the nature of true Christianity, so the Quran itself is in error in commending the Bible, which in turn undermines it as a true revelation from God. If it were a true revelation from God, it would have recognized the true nature of Christianity to begin with.[19]

The "Many Versions" of the Bible

The argument that there are many versions of the Bible but only one version of the Quran is hollow because the argument does not accurately reflect the facts. We do not have different versions of the Bible in the sense of having different Bibles (with different books, chapters, and verses); rather we have different translations from the same basic set of Hebrew and Greek manuscripts in our possession. Such translations include the New American Standard Version, the New International Version, and the King James Version.

A number of English translations of the Quran are available, but no one refers to "different versions" of the Quran. Likewise, we have different translations of the Bible, but they are all based on the same body of Hebrew and Greek manuscripts.

Four Thousand Gospels?

As noted previously, Muslim apologist Ahmed Deedat argues that "out of over four thousand differing manuscripts the Christians boast about, the church fathers just selected four which tallied with their prejudices and called them Gospels of Matthew, Mark, Luke and John."[20] Deedat completely misunderstands the nature of the biblical manuscripts. The thousands of manuscripts we possess are copies of all 27 books of the New Testament. Many of these manuscripts are copies of the four canonical Gospels. Such an embarrassing misunderstanding on Deedat's part shows he has not carefully examined the evidence.

Eyewitness Testimony in the New Testament

Contrary to the claim of Muslim apologist Maurice Bucaille that "we do not in fact have an eyewitness account from the life of Jesus,"[21] the New Testament is based on eyewitness testimony. For example, John, who wrote the Gospel of John, said in his first epistle, "That which was from the beginning, which we have heard, which we have seen with our eyes, which we have looked at and our hands have touched—this we proclaim concerning the Word of life" (1 John 1:1). John was with Jesus' mother, Mary, at the foot of the cross as Jesus was dying (John 19:16-17). Peter, though not an author of a Gospel, was nevertheless an eyewitness and wrote in one of his epistles, "We did not follow cleverly invented stories when we told you about the power and coming of our Lord Jesus Christ, but we were eyewitnesses of his majesty" (2 Peter 1:16).

Apparent Contradictions, or Bible Corruption?

We can make several points in response to the Muslim claim

about contradictions in the Bible. First, the Gospels may have some apparent contradictions, but they do not have genuine contradictions. They have differences, yes, but actual contradictions, no.

Second, inspiration (the fact that Scripture is "God-breathed"— 2 Timothy 3:16) and inerrancy are, strictly speaking, ascribed only to the original autographs of Scripture. Certainly I believe the copies we have of the original autographs are extremely accurate. But theologians have been very careful to say that the Scriptures, in their original autographs and properly interpreted, will be shown to be wholly true in everything they teach.

Third, if all four Gospels were the same, with no differences, Muslim critics would be screaming collusion. The Gospel differences argue against collusion and represent four different (but inspired) accounts of the same events.

Fourth, a partial account in a biblical book is not a faulty account. One biblical book might provide some details on an event, and another biblical book might provide other, different details regarding the same event. The different details do not make the accounts faulty.

The following books will help you to convincingly resolve the vast majority of alleged Bible contradictions:

- Ron Rhodes, *What Does the Bible Say About...* (Harvest House Publishers).

- Norman Geisler and Thomas Howe, *When Critics Ask: A Popular Handbook on Bible Difficulties* (Baker Books).

- Gleason Archer, *An Encyclopedia of Bible Difficulties* (Zondervan).

- Walter C. Kaiser, *Hard Sayings of the Old Testament* (InterVarsity Press).

- Walter C. Kaiser, *More Hard Sayings of the Old Testament* (InterVarsity Press).

- Larry Richards, *Bible Difficulties Solved* (Fleming H. Revell).

- Robert H. Stein, *Difficult Passages in the New Testament* (Baker Books).

- William Arndt, *Bible Difficulties and Seeming Contradictions* (Concordia Publishing House).

- Manfred T. Brauch, *Hard Sayings of Paul* (InterVarsity Press).

- F.F. Bruce, *Hard Sayings of Jesus* (InterVarsity Press).

- John W. Haley, *Alleged Discrepancies of the Bible* (Baker Books).

By studying such books, an objective person will grow in leaps and bounds in his or her confidence in the reliability of the Bible. Muslims will find such books real eye-openers.

WAS JESUS MERELY A PROPHET?

MUSLIMS BELIEVE JESUS was one of the foremost prophets of Allah. He was a sinless man who was a messenger of God, bringing truth for His age. He was not the Son of God, nor was He God in human flesh. He was not a partner of God, for that would constitute blasphemy against Allah.

Muslims give Jesus great honor, but not more than is due any other prophet of Allah. Jesus Himself said in the Quran: "Lo! I am the slave of Allah. He hath given me the Scripture and hath appointed me a Prophet" (Sura 19:30). The Quran calls Him a lesser prophet than Muhammad.

THE MUSLIM VIEW OF JESUS

An Apostle or Prophet of Allah

Innumerable verses in the Christian Bible deal with the person of Jesus, but only a sparse 74 verses out of 6236 in the Quran deal with Him—and of those, some 42 are indirect references.[1] Jesus is obviously not a major player in the Quran.

One of the more central Quranic verses is Sura 4:171: "Christ Jesus the son of Mary was (no more than) an apostle of God, and His Word, which He bestowed on Mary." Muslims believe this verse is rich in commendations for Jesus. For example, He is called an apostle—essentially, a prophet—of Allah, even though He is a much lesser prophet than Muhammad. Muslims say Jesus never claimed to be more than a prophet. Indeed, He is just one among many thousands (allegedly 124,000) prophets of Allah. He is great, but He is not unique.

Sura 3:45 tells us that Jesus' name is "the Messiah" (see also Sura 4:157,171). Again, however, Muslims do not mean by *Messiah* what Christians do. In fact, Muslims seem to have no awareness of the true significance of this term, and they certainly have no conception of the Messiah as a divine being. The Quran warns the "people of the book" (that is, Christians) not to consider Jesus as more than a messenger from God: "The Messiah, son of Mary, was no other than a messenger, messengers (the like of whom) had passed away before him" (Sura 5:75). Jesus was born of the Virgin Mary by a special miracle (Sura 3:47). Muslim theologian Zamakhsari says Mary conceived "when the angel Gabriel blew up her garment."[2]

A Miracle Worker

Muslims highly revere Jesus for the miracles He performed (Sura 3:49). The Quran teaches that Jesus took some clay and "didst blow upon it and it was a bird" (Sura 5:110). He also "didst heal him who was born blind and the leper" and "didst raise the dead" (Sura 5:110).

Muslims think it is wonderful that Jesus healed sick people and raised dead people to life. Even to this day, if a person wishes to compliment a doctor in Iran, he may say something like this: "Doctor, you perform miracles; you have the breath of Jesus!"[3] Yet Muslims do not see miracles as proof that Jesus was a divine being or that He was the Son of God. They suggest Allah enabled Jesus to do such things.

Jesus the Son of God?

Muslims argue that Jesus was not the Son of God. They say people who believe Jesus is the Son of God are deluded (Sura 9:30). In Muslim thinking, the suggestion that Jesus was the Son of God implies that Allah had sexual relations with a female partner (Mary), which yielded the birth of Jesus. The Quran is clear, however, that Allah has no consort: "How can He have a son when He hath no consort?" (Sura 6:101). The Quran also states of Allah, "No son has He begotten, nor has He a partner in His dominion" (Sura 25:2). Further, we are told that "He begetteth not, nor is He begotten" (Sura 112:3).

One Muslim apologist says, "The Muslim takes exception to the word 'begotten,' because begetting is an animal act, belonging to the lower animal functions of sex. How can we attribute such a lowly capacity to God?"[4]

Further, Muslims say, if Jesus was the Son of God, why did He so often claim to be merely the Son of Man? Jesus' own words argue against the idea that He was the Son of God.[5]

Jesus Was Not God

Muslims are emphatic that Jesus was not an incarnation of God in human flesh. Christians who hold to such an idea are guilty of blasphemy (Sura 5:17,73). To say Jesus was God would be to acknowledge more than one God, which constitutes a denial of Islam's basic confession that there is only one God whose name is Allah (see Sura 5:116-117). Christians who make such a claim are infidels, for such a view greatly dishonors Allah.

One Muslim apologist goes so far as to say the Christian Bible does not contain a single unequivocal statement where Jesus claimed to be God or where He instructed His followers to worship Him.[6] Jesus never claimed to be more than a prophet.

Jesus' Crucifixion

The Quran states that Jesus did not die by crucifixion, but He was made to appear to die in that manner (Sura 4:157). How did this work? Muslims offer a variety of explanations. Some Muslims argue that the Roman guards seized and arrested the wrong Jesus— Barabbas (tradition says he was also named Jesus)—and crucified him. We are told that when Jesus encountered the disciples on the road to Emmaus (Luke 24), He was actually seeking to escape from Jerusalem before anyone discovered the error in arresting the wrong Jesus.[7]

Another popular theory is that Judas was crucified on the cross. According to this theory, after Judas betrayed Jesus, Allah transformed Judas so that he looked like Jesus, and then Judas was nailed to the cross to die. Jesus, unharmed, was then taken directly into heaven.[8] The Quran says, "Allah took him up unto Himself" (Sura 4:158). This raising to heaven was not the ascension that the Bible records (Acts 1:9-11). Rather, Jesus was transferred into God's presence without experiencing death in much the same way that Elijah was.

What is the reason for such theories "proving" that Jesus never died by crucifixion? In Muslim thinking, Allah would never desert a prophet (like Jesus) in the fulfillment of his mission and allow him to die a degrading death. For Jesus to die on a cross would be contrary to Allah's omnipotence, who would surely rescue a prophet in danger. Muslims sometimes argue that they honor Jesus more than Christians do because death by crucifixion would be a dishonor. They say Allah honored Jesus by taking Him straight to heaven.

Muslim apologists claim that Jesus never said, "I was dead and now I'm alive." We are told, "Throughout the length and breadth of the 27 books of the New Testament, there is not a single statement made by Jesus Christ that 'I was dead, and I have come back from the dead.'"[9]

Jesus' Resurrection

In Luke 24:39 Jesus told His disciples, "Look at my hands and my feet. It is I myself! Touch me and see; a ghost does not have flesh and bones, as you see I have." Muslim apologists believe this verse proves Jesus did not die and therefore was not resurrected from the dead. A Muslim paraphrase of the verse might be this: "What is wrong with you disciples? Can't you see I am the same person who walked and talked with you, broke bread with you, flesh and blood in all respects?"[10] Jesus was simply telling the disciples that they should touch Him and handle Him so they could see He had not died and been resurrected in a spiritualized body. He was still physically alive and in their midst.

In keeping with this, as noted previously, Muslims argue that there was no ascension of a resurrected Jesus. They claim that the authors of the four canonical Gospels did not record a single word about the ascension of Jesus.[11]

The Second Coming of Jesus

Muslims believe that one day Jesus will come back to earth, slay all who do not accept Islam as the one true religion, reign for 40 years, and then die and be buried next to Muhammad in Medina. Following this He will be resurrected with all other men and women on the last day.

A CHRISTIAN RESPONSE

Jesus, the Son of God

If Muslims were right in saying the term "Son of God" demanded that God have sexual relations with a female, the doctrine would cause Christians to shrink back in horror every bit as much as Muslims do. But the Bible contains no such idea. The Bible indicates Jesus is *eternally* the Son of God.

Among the ancients, the term *son of* often metaphorically meant "of the order of." The Old Testament often uses the phrase this way. "Sons of the prophets" meant "of the order of prophets" (1 Kings 20:35). "Sons of the singers" meant "of the order of singers" (Nehemiah 12:28 NASB). Likewise, the phrase "Son of God" means "of the order of God," and represents a claim to undiminished deity. The phrase includes no sexual connotation.

Ancient Semites and Asians used the phrase "son of" to indicate likeness or sameness of nature and equality of being. When Jesus claimed to be the Son of God, His Jewish contemporaries fully understood He was making a claim to be God in an unqualified sense.

We have plenty of evidence for Christ's eternal Sonship. God created the universe through His Son—implying Christ was the Son of God prior to the creation (Hebrews 1:2). Moreover, Christ as the Son existed "before all things" (Colossians 1:17). As well, Jesus, speaking as the Son of God (John 8:54-56), asserts His eternal pre-existence before Abraham (verse 58).

So the Muslim view constitutes a gross misunderstanding of the title. World religions scholar Dean Halverson shows how different Arab words for "son of" can help explain the correct meaning of "Son of God":

> In the Arabic language there are two words for expressing "Son of": *walad* and *ibn*. *Walad* definitely denotes becoming a son through the union of a male with a female. We as Christians would agree that Jesus was not a *waladdu'llah*—"Son of God"—in that sense...Unlike *walad*, however, the word *ibn* can be used in a metaphorical sense. For example, Arabs themselves talk about a traveler as being an *ibnu'ssabil*—"Son of the road." They obviously do not mean by such a phrase that one has had sexual relations with the road. It is in this wider metaphorical sense that Jesus is understood as being the Son of God.[12]

What about the Muslim retort that Christ is said to be "begotten" in the New Testament (John 1:14,18 KJV). Actually, the Greek word for *begotten (monogenes)* does not mean Christ was procreated but rather means "unique" or "one of a kind." Jesus is the Son of God in the sense that He uniquely has the same nature as the Father—a divine nature.

Jesus, the Son of Man

If Jesus was the Son of God, Muslims ask, why did He say He was the Son of Man (Matthew 20:18; 24:30)? This is not a contradiction, for Jesus was both the Son of God *and* the Son of Man. Even if the phrase "Son of Man" were solely a reference to Jesus' humanity, it would not constitute a denial of His deity. In becoming a human being, Jesus did not cease to be God. Christ's Incarnation did not involve the subtraction of deity but the addition of humanity. Jesus clearly asserted His deity on many occasions (Matthew 16:16-17; John 8:58; 10:30). But besides being divine, He had a human nature in the Incarnation (see Philippians 2:6-8). He thus had two natures (divine and human) conjoined in one person.

Scripture itself indicates Jesus was not denying He was God when He referred to Himself as the Son of Man. The term "Son of Man" is used of Christ in contexts where His deity is quite evident. For example, the Bible indicates that only God has the prerogative of forgiving sins (Isaiah 43:25), but Jesus referred to Himself as the Son of Man when He exercised this prerogative (Mark 2:7-10). Likewise, at the second coming, Christ will return to earth as the Son of Man in clouds of glory to reign on earth (Matthew 26:63-64). Jesus, the Son of Man, is the divine Messiah.

Jesus' Deity

A comparison of the Old and New Testaments provides powerful testimony to Jesus' identity as Yahweh (God Almighty). For example, the Old Testament indicates that only God saves. In Isaiah 43:11, God asserts, "I, even I, am the LORD [Yahweh], and apart from me there is no savior." This is an extremely important verse, for it indicates that (1) a claim to be Savior is a claim to deity, and (2) there is only one Savior—God. Against this backdrop, the New Testament reveals Christ's divine nature by referring to Jesus as the Savior (Titus 2:13-14).

Likewise, God says in Isaiah 44:24, "I, the LORD [Yahweh], am the maker of all things, stretching out the heavens by Myself, and spreading out the earth all alone." The fact that Yahweh is the maker of all things who stretched out the heavens by Himself and spread out the earth all alone—and the accompanying fact that Christ is the Creator of all things (John 1:3; Colossians 1:16; Hebrews 1:2)—proves that Christ is God Almighty.

Certainly a clear indicator of Jesus' deity is the fact that divine names are consistently ascribed to Him in the Bible. We have seen that Jesus is equated with the Yahweh of the Old Testament. But the New Testament equivalent of *Yahweh* is *Kurios*. Like *Yahweh, Kurios* means "Lord" and usually carries the idea of a sovereign being who exercises absolute authority.

The apostle Paul points us to the close relationship between *Yahweh* and *Kurios* in Philippians 2. He tells us that Christ was given a name above every name, "that at the name of Jesus every knee should bow, in heaven and on earth and under the earth, and every tongue confess that Jesus Christ is Lord [Kurios]" (verses 10-11). Paul, an Old Testament scholar par excellence, is alluding to Isaiah 45:22-24: "I am God, and there is no other. By myself I have sworn, my mouth has uttered in all integrity a word that will not be revoked: Before me every knee will bow; by me every tongue will swear." Paul was drawing on his vast knowledge of the Old Testament to make the point that Jesus Christ is Yahweh, the Lord (Kurios) of all mankind.

What about the Muslim claim that Jesus never instructed His followers to worship Him? Actually, many people worshipped Jesus in the New Testament, and He always accepted their worship as perfectly appropriate. Jesus received worship from Thomas (John 20:28), the angels (Hebrews 1:6), some wise men (Matthew 2:11), a leper (Matthew 8:2), a ruler (Matthew 9:18), a blind man (John 9:38), an anonymous woman (Matthew 15:25), Mary Magdalene (Matthew 28:9), and the disciples (Matthew 28:17).

Jesus' Miracles

Though Muslims say Jesus' miracles do not signify His divine identity, the Bible says His miracles *do* signify His identity. Scripture often refers to the miracles of Jesus as "signs." This word emphasizes the significance of the action rather than the marvel (see John 4:54; 6:14; 9:16). Jesus strategically performed these signs to signify His true identity and glory as the divine Messiah (see Isaiah 29:18-21; 35:5-6; 61:1-2). His miracles served as His divine credentials—His divine ID card, so to speak.

Jesus, the Supreme Prophet

Jesus *was* a prophet (Matthew 13:53-57). Notice, however, that as a prophet, Jesus' teachings were always ultimate and final. He never wavered in this. Jesus unflinchingly placed His teachings above those of Moses and the prophets—and in a Jewish culture at that!

Jesus always spoke in His own authority. He never said, "Thus saith the Lord" as did the common prophets (or "Allah says," as did Muhammad). He always said, "Verily, verily, I say unto you" (KJV). He never retracted anything He said, never guessed or spoke with uncertainty, never made revisions, never contradicted Himself (as Muhammad did), never resorted to abrogations (as Allah did), and never apologized for what He said. He even asserted that "heaven and earth will pass away, but my words will not pass away" (Mark 13:31), thus elevating His words directly to the realm of heaven.

One cannot read the Gospels long before recognizing that Jesus regarded Himself and His message as inseparable. Jesus' teachings have ultimate authority because He is God. The words of Jesus are the very words of God (see John 3:34)!

Moreover, Jesus was not just a prophet to Israel, as Muslims claim. His words were intended for the whole world. In His great commission to the disciples, Jesus said, "All authority in heaven and on earth has been given to me. Therefore go and make disciples of all nations" (Matthew 28:18-19).

Still further, contrary to the Muslim claim that each prophet's truth abrogates revelation from previous prophets, Jesus denied that He abrogated revelations from earlier prophets. Indeed, He said in Matthew 5:17-18, "Do not think that I have come to abolish the Law or the Prophets; I have not come to abolish them but to fulfill them. I tell you the truth, until heaven and earth disappear, not the smallest letter, not the least stroke of a pen, will by any means disappear from the Law until everything is accomplished."

Jesus also indicated His own words would never, ever be abrogated. Jesus flatly asserted, "Heaven and earth will pass away, but my words will never pass away" (Matthew 24:35). This means that nothing Muhammad said could ever abrogate or do away with Jesus' words. Jesus' words are final and authoritative because He Himself is God.

Jesus' Death on the Cross

The Muslim charge that Jesus did not die on a cross lacks historical support. However, the Bible provides substantial evidence that Jesus died on the cross:

- The Old Testament includes numerous predictions about Jesus' death (Psalm 22:16; Isaiah 53:5-10; Daniel 9:26; Zechariah 12:10).

- The Bible contains many predictions that Jesus would be resurrected (see Psalm 16:10; Matthew 12:40; 17:22-23; John 2:19-21), but He could not be resurrected without first dying.

- Jesus often spoke of the fact that He was going to die for the sins of humankind (Matthew 12:40; Mark 8:31; John 2:19-21; 10:10-11).

- Jesus' own mother and His beloved disciple John were eye-witnesses of His crucifixion (John 19:16-17).

- Jesus was beaten almost beyond recognition by Roman guards, given a crown of thorns, and then crucified. He bled from large wounds to His hands and feet, losing a phenomenal amount of blood. He was stabbed in the side with a spear, causing "blood and water" to flow (John 19:34). No one could survive such wounds.

- At the last moment of life, Jesus gave up His spirit to the Father (Luke 23:46-49).

- Pilate checked to make sure Jesus was dead (Mark 15:44-45).

- Ancient non-Christian historians also recorded Christ's death as a fact. This includes such notables as the Roman historian Cornelius Tacitus and Jewish historian Flavius Josephus. Early Christian writers like Polycarp affirmed Christ's death.

God the Father Allowed Jesus to Die

Muslims claim Allah would never have allowed one of his own prophets to be dishonored and to suffer a humiliating death on a cross. The crucifixion is simply incompatible with Allah's absolute sovereignty.

Contrary to this view, the Bible is clear that God Himself allowed Jesus to die on the cross for the salvation of humankind (Romans 8:3-4; 1 Peter 1:18-20). Clearly, God often allows His servants (whether prophets, apostles, or His own Son) to suffer. God's sovereignty is not incompatible with His allowance of certain events that, from our limited perspective, seem unfair or bad. The story of Job is a profound example (read chapters 1–3). Even Muhammad suffered to some extent. Indeed, some accounts indicate he died from the poison of one of his wives, a Jewess.[13]

Besides, who is to say God did not rescue Jesus from His enemies? Norman Geisler and Abdul Saleeb make the keen observation that "even if Muslims assume that God will deliver his prophets from their enemies, it is wrong to conclude that he did not deliver Christ from his enemies. Indeed, this is precisely what the resurrection is."[14]

As we noted earlier in the book, *Islam* means "submission." *Muslim* means "one who submits." Jesus was One who submitted. Indeed, He submitted in obedience to God all the way to the cross (Hebrews 5:7-9). Muslims should therefore honor Jesus for this great act of submission, for by it, He attained the salvation of humankind.

Jesus' Resurrection and Ascension

Jesus not only rose from the dead but also provided powerful evidence for the resurrection before many witnesses. Scripture tells us that Jesus first attested to His resurrection by appearing to Mary Magdalene (John 20:1)—a fact which is a highly significant indicator of the authenticity and reliability of the resurrection account. The disciples could not have fabricated the resurrection story, for no one in a first-century Jewish culture would have invented it this way. A woman's testimony was unacceptable in any Jewish court of law except in a very few circumstances. A fabricator would have been much more likely to place Peter or the other male disciples at the resurrection tomb. But our biblical text tells us that the Lord appeared first to Mary because in fact that was the way it actually happened.

Moreover, by all accounts, the disciples came away from the crucifixion frightened and full of doubt. And yet, following Jesus' resurrection appearance to the disciples, their lives were transformed. They became bulwarks of courage, fearless defenders of the faith. Only the resurrection could account for this incredible transformation. These witnesses gave up their lives defending the truth of the resurrection and Christianity.

As the days passed, Jesus continued to make many appearances and proved that He indeed had risen from the dead. Acts 1:3 says, "He showed himself to these men and gave many convincing proofs that he was alive. He appeared to them over a period of forty days and spoke about the kingdom of God." Moreover, "He appeared to more than five hundred of the brothers at the same time, most of whom are still living" (1 Corinthians 15:6).

What about the Muslim argument against the death and resurrection of Christ from Luke 24:39, where Jesus said, "Look at my hands and my feet. It is I myself! Touch me and see; a ghost does not have flesh and bones, as you see I have"? Muslims believe Jesus was telling the disciples they should touch Him and handle Him so they could see He had not died but was still physically alive and in their midst. The folly of this view is clear because immediately following Jesus' words in Luke 24:39, He goes on to explain that He indeed had risen from the dead in fulfillment of the Scriptures: "This is what is written: The Christ will suffer and rise from the dead on the third day, and repentance and forgiveness of sins will be preached in his name to all nations, beginning at Jerusalem" (Luke 24:46-47). Muslims are ripping verses out of context in an attempt to prove a futile point.

Muslims are also wrong in the claim that "nowhere in the 27 books of the New Testament did Jesus ever say He was dead and now alive." Early in Luke's Gospel, Jesus affirmed, "The Son of Man must suffer many things and be rejected by the elders, chief priests and teachers of the law, and he must be killed and on the third day be raised to life" (Luke 9:22). Jesus later told His disciples, "This is what is written: The Christ will suffer and rise from the dead on the third day" (Luke 24:46). Further, in the book of Revelation, the resurrected Christ claimed, "I am the Living One; I was dead, and behold I am alive for ever and ever!" (Revelation 1:18).

Ahmed Deedat is wrong yet again in arguing that the canonical Gospel writers never recorded a single word about the ascension of Christ. In John 20:17, we read Christ's own words: "I am ascending to my Father and to your Father, to my God and to your God." In John 7:33 Jesus said, "I am with you for only a short time, and then I go to the one who sent me." "Now I am going to him who sent me" (John 16:5). "I am going to the Father, where you can see me no longer" (John 16:10). In Acts 1:9, Luke (the same author who wrote the Gospel of Luke) writes, "He was taken up before their very eyes, and a cloud hid him from their sight" (Acts 1:9).

Some Muslim apologists erroneously make bold claims about the Bible, so I urge you to never take their word for what the Bible says, but always open up your Bible and check it out for yourself. Muslims have offered some futile arguments against the resurrection and ascension of Jesus Christ, but the fact is that Jesus is missing from His tomb while Muhammad's tomb is still occupied at a mosque in Medina.[15] In terms of eternal salvation, Muslims would do well to place their faith in the Living One who was dead but is now alive for ever and ever! (Revelation 1:18).

10

DIALOGUING WITH MUSLIMS

WITNESSING TO MUSLIMS can be a trying experience. But you can greatly enhance your effectiveness in dialoguing with them by deciding in advance to handle your witnessing encounters in a certain way. Following are some suggestions.

ALWAYS PREPARE BY PRAYER

Pray regularly about your witnessing opportunities. Remember, only God in His mighty power can lift the veil of spiritual blindness from the human heart (John 8:32; 2 Corinthians 3:16; 4:4). Pray fervently and often for the Muslims you witness to (Luke 18:1-8; James 5:16).

I especially appreciate Acts 16:14 in this regard: "One of those listening [to Paul speaking] was a woman named Lydia, a dealer in purple cloth from the city of Thyatira, who was a worshipper of God. The Lord opened her heart to respond to Paul's message." When praying for a Muslim, pray that the Lord would open his or her heart to the gospel of Jesus Christ. He has the power to do it.

DEVELOP PERSONAL RELATIONSHIPS

You may have a Muslim friend or family member. In that case, you've already got a lot going for you, because personal relationships are very important to success in witnessing. If the Muslim to whom you want to witness is someone you encounter socially, and you do not yet have a personal relationship, try to develop one.

A sincere friendship characterized by trust and compassion can earn you the right to be heard.[1] Christian writer Phil Parshall says he has found in his long experience that Muslims typically become attracted to Christianity through the life and witness of a person who takes the time and effort to cultivate a genuine friendship.[2] John Gilchrist agrees, adding that "Muslims are unlikely to become your *brethren* until they first become your *friends*."[3] By building and developing friendships with Muslims, Christians lay a strong foundation for an effective witness.

BE LOVING

When witnessing to Muslims, Christians should do all they can to let the love of Christ shine through them (see 1 Corinthians 16:14; Ephesians 5:2; 1 Timothy 4:12). William Miller, well experienced in witnessing to Muslims, observes that many Muslims who have converted to Christianity say the thing that got their attention is the Christlike love of Christians.[4]

ARGUMENTS WITHOUT QUARRELS

In many Arab countries, a heated debate with someone is considered something that adds a little spice to life. Many times Muslims can become quite animated in such debates, and unless the more soft-spoken Westerner is aware that this is common among Muslims, he might feel uncomfortable continuing the discussion. My point in bringing this up is that should your dialogue become a debate and your Muslim acquaintance become animated, just keep your cool. If you sense it is fine to continue, keep making your points in a calm way without succumbing to raising your voice. Your debate with the Muslim should be charitable, tactful, and friendly (2 Timothy 2:24).

A COMMITTED CHRISTIAN LIFESTYLE

Simply speaking nice words about Christianity is not enough. The Muslim must see that the life you live is a reflection of your beliefs. If he sees an inconsistency between your mouth and your life, your words will carry little weight. One of the best ways to dispel the stereotypes many Muslims have about Christians is to truly "walk the walk" in a committed relationship with Jesus. A deeply committed Christian life will be like a fragrance that draws people to Christ. The way you live will either open or close the door for further discussions with a Muslim acquaintance.

ONE ON ONE

Witnessing to Muslims is best done on a one-to-one basis. Muslims are generally vigorous and dutiful in their defense of Islam when they are with other Muslims.[5] In a group setting, individual Muslims will not feel the freedom to express any doubts they have about Islam, and they will be fearful of asking questions about Christianity. This makes evangelism nearly impossible. To avoid this problem, speak to a single Muslim at a time.

BEWARE OF STEREOTYPES

Muslims and Christians have stereotypes of each other. Unless you recognize and deal with these stereotypes, they can erect unnecessary and troublesome barriers to communication.

- Many Muslims believe Westerners are materialistic, immoral (sexually free, intemperate, racist), do not value life (too many abortions), do not value the family unit, pay little respect to the elderly, and show too few moral standards regarding television and movies.

- Many Christians believe Muslims are all Arabs, many are rich oil sheiks, most of them are extremists and terrorists, and they are generally sinister and dangerous people.

- Many Christians believe they don't know enough and are not qualified to reach Muslims for Christ.

• Muslims believe they are very religious people following the truth and are enlightened with the true religion.[6]

When Christians encounter Muslims who argue for the supremacy of Islam by slamming Christianity—equating it with Western degeneracy—the Christian can distinguish between Christianity and the vices of the West. Christians must point out that the West has succumbed to so many vices not because the West is Christian but because the West has largely ignored Christianity. Christians can also point out that such vices illustrate one of the primary teachings of Christianity—that humankind is engulfed in a serious sin problem.

Muslims sometimes back Christians into a corner by asking them, "Are you a Christian?" If the Christian says yes, without qualifying his answer, the Muslim will likely assume he is a person of low morals. As Sobhi Malek points out, most Muslims use the word *Christian* to mean "someone who comes from a culture which is broadly labeled as 'Christian'...Muslims often associate with the term 'Christian' the things that born-again believers from the West often associate with the term 'non-Christian'!"[7] Malek suggests handling the discussion in this way:

> Muslim: Are you a Christian?
>
> Missionary: What do you mean by "Christian"?
>
> Muslim: I mean Westerner, European, non-Muslim, someone who does not follow the teachings of the Quran. I mean someone with low morals like the people I see in the movies and read about in the books that come from Europe and the United States.
>
> Missionary: If that is what you mean, my answer is no. In fact, I was that kind of person you have described, but I've been converted! Now I follow Christ according to the Bible.[8]

NOT ALL MUSLIMS ARE MILITANT

To conclude that all Muslims are militant and hostile toward Western civilization would be foolish. Most media reports about Muslims focus attention on extremists who are engaged in terrorism.

Unfortunately, this brings unfair bad press for mainstream Muslims living in the United States. As Donald Tingle points out, "these news stories of extremist activities by a minority of Arabs in one part of the world distort the overall picture of Islam...In a study of any religion we must step beyond the extremist activities of a few and view the religion as a whole."[9]

I recall that just after 9/11, a kindly Muslim family showed up at our church on a Sunday morning to give flowers to the pastoral staff as an act of compassion. Their loving expression drew a wide line in the sand between them and the Muslim terrorists responsible for the tragedies in New York, Washington, and Pennsylvania.

Many Muslims in the United States are very good friends and neighbors. They are loving and hospitable people, and they are open to discussing their faith with you.

LEARN ABOUT ISLAM

The Christian who seeks to witness to Muslims should learn as much about Islam as possible. He should learn something of the history of Muhammad, the doctrines taught in the Quran, and the practices Muslims engage in. A Christian ought also to read at least the first two chapters of the Quran so he can honestly say he has read part of it.

Only when a Christian understands some of these factors will he be able to intelligently share the gospel of Christ with a Muslim. Such an understanding of Islam will also help him avoid misunderstandings with a Muslim. For example, the informed Christian will not call Jesus the Son of God without qualifying that this does not mean the Father had a sexual partner, but rather that this is a figurative expression that describes the eternal relationship between the Father and Jesus.

A Muslim will respect you for going to the trouble of learning about Islam. He will take you much more seriously.

AVOID CRITICISM

It is not wise to start off your conversation with a Muslim by slamming Muhammad, Allah, or the Quran. Coming right out and saying Muhammad is a false prophet who spoke of a false God will only serve to close the Muslim's mind and create a huge barrier. Your conversation will essentially be over if you start out by saying bad things about someone (or something) he has revered his entire life. You may win an argument but lose a friend. Especially early on in your discussions, focus attention on a positive presentation of the Bible, Jesus, and His gospel of grace.[10]

If a Muslim asks you early on what you think of the Quran, you might say, "I agree with the Quran in every place that it is in agreement with the Christian Bible." Then emphasize why you believe in the Bible.

If a Muslim asks you early on what you think of Muhammad, you might say, "I respect Muhammad as a leader of the Arab people and as one who took a stand against idolatry. But as a Christian, I am a follower of Jesus Christ, the Lamb of God who died for my sins. Now I have an assurance of eternal life. May I tell you about that assurance?"[11]

As your relationship develops and you grow to trust each other's motives and become more comfortable with each other, you can tactfully and gracefully focus attention on concerns you have about Muhammad, the Quran, and other Islamic distinctives.

DEFINE YOUR TERMS

Muslims often refer to God, Jesus, the Holy Spirit, prayer, the angels, and other terms common to the Bible, but they attach entirely different meanings to these words. This means that when they use these terms, you may not understand what they mean by what they are saying. Likewise, when you use such terms, they will likely not interpret your words the way you are intending. This is known as a *terminology block*. Unless you define your terms biblically and overcome the terminology block, little true communication will take place.

ASK LEADING QUESTIONS

You will not be able to force your opinion on a Muslim. But if you can help the Muslim discover problems in the Quran and in Islamic theology for himself, you will have accomplished a good thing.

One great way to help a Muslim discover problems in his viewpoint is by asking strategic questions, all the while remaining tactful and kind. Remember, Jesus often asked questions to make a point (see Luke 9:20).

> Rather than shower his listeners with information, [Jesus] used questions to draw answers out of them. A person can close his ears to facts he doesn't want to hear, but if a pointed question causes him to form the answer in his own mind, he cannot escape the conclusion—because it's a conclusion that he reached himself.[12]

So, for example, you might ask your Muslim acquaintance, "Do you know for sure you will go to paradise when you die?" (Muslims have no assurance of salvation, so the Muslim will probably say no.) Then you can ask, "Have you considered Jesus' words about how His followers can be sure that they are saved? What do you think He meant when He said, 'I give them eternal life, and they shall never perish; no one can snatch them out of my hand' (John 10:28)?"

By tactfully asking such questions, you can cause the Muslim to think for himself about issues that may open his heart to the truth of the Bible.

QUOTE THE BIBLE

Do not hesitate to quote the Bible. Remember, "Faith comes by hearing, and hearing by the word of God" (Romans 10:17 KJV). The psalmist affirmed, "The unfolding of your words gives light; it gives understanding to the simple" (Psalm 119:130). If you plant the seed of the Word of God in good soil (the heart of an open-minded Muslim), you may soon be seeing some fruit! As a practical matter, I advise using an easy-to-understand Bible translation when witnessing. As you share from the Bible, pray that the Holy Spirit will bear witness to the truth of God's Word in your friend's heart (1 Corinthians 2:9-12).

Keep in mind that because of cultural differences, men should help men understand the Bible, and women should help women. Ergun Mehmet Caner and Emir Fethi Caner offer this advice:

> Most Islamic culture strongly forbids casual conversation with a member of the opposite sex. To cross this boundary may be viewed as insulting in a Muslim family. For a woman to speak forcefully to a man shows disrespect, and a Christian man who speaks to a Muslim woman without her husband present insults the husband. American Islam tends to be less restrictive, but Christians should observe conversation protocols until they discern that it is safe to do otherwise.[13]

Be sure to show a high level of respect for your Bible. Muslims show great respect for the Quran by not placing anything on top of it and by keeping it at the highest place in the house. Do not throw your Bible under your chair after you finish sharing. Muslims do not write in the Quran, so when you share from the Bible, you might want to use one you haven't written in. (They might consider writing in the Bible disrespectful, or they may think you are adding to the Word of God.)

RECOMMEND A GOSPEL

If you can afford to, give your Muslim acquaintance a copy of the New Testament and ask him or her to read through the Gospel of Luke. After all, this Gospel already contains themes the Muslim is familiar with, such as the angel's announcement to Mary that she would bear Jesus and the birth of John the Baptist. Such familiar ground may put the Muslim at ease.[14]

Another great thing about Luke's Gospel is that it contains many interesting stories and parables, *and Muslims love stories!* The story of Jesus calling Levi shows that Jesus accepts people who are considered the worst of sinners (Luke 5:27-31). The parable of the lost sheep shows God rejoicing when a sinner repents, and it shows God as the aggressor in bringing lost people to Himself (Luke 15:1-7). The parable of the lost coin shows God seeking sinners and rejoicing when they turn to Him (Luke 15:8-10). The parable of the prodigal son demonstrates how wide open God's arms are to those who err and then come back to Him (Luke 15:11-24).[15] Such stories will be highly meaningful to the Muslim. You can use these stories as launchpads to share the gospel.

EMPHASIZE THE LOVE OF GOD

God is not just characterized by love. He is the very personification of love (1 John 4:8). Love permeates His being. And God's love does not depend upon the lovability of the object (human beings). God loves us despite the fact that we are fallen in sin (John 3:16-21). (God loves the sinner even though He hates the sin.)

One of the wonderful teachings of the New Testament is that "God demonstrates his own love for us in this: While we were still sinners, Christ died for us" (Romans 5:8). "This is how we know what love is: Jesus Christ laid down his life for us" (1 John 3:16). Muslims desperately need to understand that unlike Allah, the biblical God is not angry with them but is full of love for them. One Muslim who converted to Christianity explains:

> There is much fear in Islam because God is not recognized as a loving father. Once the Muslim has a real taste of the divine love of God the Father, all his fear will vanish, and he will be ready to be introduced to the salvation available for him through Jesus Christ—God the Son.[16]

EMPHASIZE GOD'S WONDERFUL GRACE

Muslims believe in a works-oriented salvation, so we can share with them what the Bible says about this. Romans 3:20 tells us, "Therefore no one will be declared righteous in his sight by observing the law; rather, through the law we become conscious of sin." Emphasize the grace of God: "For it is by grace you have been saved, through faith—and this not from yourselves, it is the gift of God—not by works, so that no one can boast" (Ephesians 2:8-9).

Try to show the futility of trying to live a life good enough to earn

God's favor. According to the Bible, even the smallest failure brings condemnation. "Whoever keeps the whole law and yet stumbles in one point, he has become guilty of all" (James 2:10). This is why God's grace is so wonderful. Salvation is literally a free gift for those who trust in Christ.

GENTLY CORRECT MISINTERPRETATIONS ABOUT JESUS

The Quran speaks about Jesus' virgin birth, His miraculous ability to heal people and raise them from the dead, the fact that He is the Messiah, that He is a word from God, that He is an all-righteous one, that He was sinless, and that He will one day return to the earth (for example, Suras 3:45; 4:158). The problem is, Muslims generally interpret these things much differently than do Christians. Use these statements from the Quran as a launch-pad to correct their misconceptions about Jesus in these areas.

For example, you might point out that in the Gospel of John the miracles of Jesus are always called signs because *signs signify something*—in this case, that Jesus is the promised divine Messiah. In Isaiah 35, the prophet said that when the divine Messiah came, He would cause lame people to walk, deaf people to hear, and blind people to see. Jesus fulfilled these specific prophecies, thereby showing He truly is the divine Messiah.

You might also point out that whereas Muhammad was exhorted in the Quran to seek forgiveness for his faults (Suras 16:61; 40:55; 42:5,30; 47:19; 48:1-2), Jesus was sinless (Hebrews 4:15) and came to solve humankind's sin dilemma (2 Corinthians 5:19-21). You might acknowledge that you are aware *you* are a sinner, and you want to make sure that the Person to whom you entrust your eternal destiny is sinless.

Finally, as noted earlier in the book, *Islam* literally means "submission." Emphasize that Jesus submitted in going to the cross for the sins of humankind, making possible a free gift of salvation for those who believe in Him (Hebrews 5:7-9). Surely such submission is worthy of honor.

SOME PRACTICAL MATTERS

Wear appropriate clothes. If you have a Muslim over to your house, ask your wife and daughters to dress modestly with clothing that does not draw attention to the female figure.

Serve appropriate food. Muslims do not eat foods that derive from swine. If you invite a Muslim over for a meal, inform him up front that you will not serve foods that are inappropriate for Muslims. You might even ask them what kind of food they would like served.

Be cautious about eye contact. Direct eye contact is not considered good manners among Muslims. If you are talking to a Muslim and he or she is constantly looking downward, understand that this is part of their culture.

Do not be offended if they don't like your pets. Muslims generally view dogs as unclean farm animals. Do not worry if they seem unimpressed with your dog. Also, beware that they might not want to shake your hand if you've just petted your animal.

Be sensitive about your hands. In Muslim culture, the left hand is used to relieve oneself (Hadith 1:155). It is therefore inappropriate to offer the left hand when shaking hands with a Muslim. The right hand is used for eating.

Do not ask a Muslim man how his wife is. This is considered inappropriate. Simply ask how the family is.

Be sensitive about shoes. In Muslim countries, Muslims often take off their shoes upon entering a door. Allow Muslims to take off their shoes in your home if they desire. Also offer to remove your shoes when you enter their home.

Be sensitive about dining preferences. Some Muslims may prefer that men eat separately from the women. Be open to this possibility.

Be sensitive regarding how meat is to be prepared. Some Muslims prefer to eat meat of an animal that has been killed in the prescribed Islamic way (in the name of Allah).

Pray with your eyes open. Muslims typically pray with their eyes open. Therefore, when giving thanks at the table, pray with your eyes open.

Do not call a Muslim "my brother." To a Muslim, this implies theological agreement. Instead, call him "my friend."

Be sensitive regarding the Muslim view of women. A whole book could be written on this topic. Here are a few facts to keep in mind: Women have far fewer rights than men do in Muslim societies. Muslim women wear a head covering, for hair can be considered an object of sexual temptation. Women are often viewed as a cause of stumbling in a man. Some Muslims believe women have less intelligence than men (Hadith 1:301). The weight of a woman's testimony is half that of man's (Hadith 1:301). A woman's salvation depends in some degree on pleasing and obeying her husband (Hadith 1:28). A Muslim man can divorce his wife without reason, but the Muslim woman has no such right. Muslim men have the right to engage in marital punishment against their wives (Sura 2:226; 4:34).

BEWARE THAT CONFLICT MAY DEVELOP

If a Muslim converts to Christianity, he can be persecuted, reviled, kicked out of his family, lose his job, and—in certain Islamic countries—put to death. Fully aware of such factors, a Muslim cannot easily become a Christian, even if he senses Christianity may be true. On the other hand, the danger of not turning to the true God is obvious.

If you sense that a Muslim is open to trusting in Christ for salvation but his fears are hindering him, gently inform him that God Himself has told us that we must always obey God above men (Acts 5:29). If God's desires conflict with what our family members say or do, we must unhesitatingly yield in obedience to God—even if this leads to disruption in the family (Matthew 10:36-39). If the Muslim *does* trust in Christ for salvation, help him or her gain a new spiritual family by introducing him or her to other Christian friends who can offer support.

BE CAUTIOUS ABOUT THE FIRST CHURCH INVITATION

Do not take Muslims to your church unless you know they are fully prepared for what they will experience. Muslims may take offence at some of what they witness at a typical church service. They will witness people putting Bibles under their chairs right next to their feet or writing in their Bibles. A man may put his arm around his wife, or teenagers may hold hands. Some people may dress more casually than seems appropriate for a church service.

Before going to a first church service, the Muslim should know what to expect so he won't be offended.[17] Do not sit a Muslim man next to a woman, for Muslims separate men and women in mosques. Explain why Christians do not take off their shoes in church the way Muslims do in a mosque. Also explain why Christians pray in church services with their eyes closed.

WITNESSING IN ARAB LANDS

I am confident that the great majority of my readers live on American soil, but I want to include a brief warning for those who may visit Arab countries. Be aware that many Arab nations consider Christian missions a crime that is severely punishable. This means that if you share Jesus Christ with Muslims in these countries, and the authorities catch you, you could end up in jail or worse. In fact, the evidence is clear that missionaries and pastors in such countries have been executed for the cause of Christ. Exercise extreme caution!

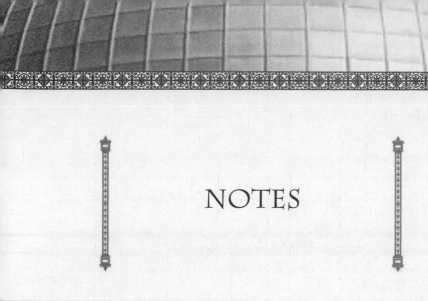

NOTES

The Global Explosion of Islam

1. Geoffrey Parrinder, *World Religions: From Ancient History to the Present* (New York: Facts on File Publications, 1971), p. 462.

2. Charles J. Adams, ed. *A Reader's Guide to the Great Religions* (New York: The Free Press, 1965), p. 287.

3. George Braswell, *What You Need to Know About Islam and Muslims* (Nashville: Broadman and Holman Publishers, 2000), p. 42.

4. David Goldmann, *Islam and the Bible: Why Two Faiths Collide* (Chicago: Moody Publishers, 2004), p. 115.

5. Braswell, p. 6.

6. Richard Bernstein, "A Growing Islamic Presence," *New York Times*, May 2, 1993, p. 1. See also John Ankerberg and John Weldon, *Fast Facts on Islam* (Eugene, OR: Harvest House Publishers, 2001), p. 13.

7. Bruce McDowell and Anees Zaka, *Muslims and Christians at the Table* (Phillipsburg, NJ: Presbyterian and Reformed Publishing, 1999), p. 8.

8. Braswell, p. 1.

9. Harold J. Berry, *Islam: What They Believe* (Lincoln, NE: Back to the Bible Publishing, 1992), p. 4.

10. Braswell, p. 1.

11. Reza F. Safa, *Inside Islam: Exposing and Reaching the World of Islam* (Lake Mary, FL: Charisma House, 1996), p. 34.

12. Safa, p. 34.

13. Braswell, p. 45.

14. Berry, p. 5.

15. Braswell, p. 2.

16. Ibid., p. 45.

17. Ibid.

18. Russell Chandler, *Racing Toward 2001* (Grand Rapids: Zondervan, 1992), p. 184.

19. William M. Miller, *A Christian's Response to Islam* (Phillipsburg, NJ: Presbyterian and Reformed Publishing, 1976), p. 94.

20. Kenneth Boa, *Cults, World Religions, and You* (Wheaton: Victor Books, 1979), p. 52.

21. Lewis M. Hopfe, *Religions of the World* (New York: Macmillan Publishers, 1991), p. 420.

22. Donald S. Tingle, *Islam and Christianity* (Downers Grove, IL: InterVarsity Press, 1985), p. 5.

23. See Braswell, p. 94.

Chapter 1—Unity and Diversity Among Muslims

1. Harold Berry, *Islam: What They Believe* (Lincoln, NE: Back to the Bible Publishing, 1992), p. 15.

2. Lewis Hopfe, *Religions of the World* (New York: Macmillan Publishers, 1991), p. 422.

3. David Goldmann, *Islam and the Bible: Why Two Faiths Collide* (Chicago: Moody Publishers, 2004), p. 15.

4. UIbid., pp. 15-16.

5. George Mather and Larry Nichols, *Dictionary of Cults, Sects, Religions and the Occult* (Grand Rapids: Zondervan, 1993), p. 141.

6. Walter Martin, *The Kingdom of the Cults* (Bloomington, MN: Bethany House Publishers, 1999), QuickVerse software.

7. Mather and Nichols, p. 141.

8. Hopfe, p. 425.

9. Dean Halverson, *The Compact Guide to World Religions* (Bloomington, MN: Bethany House Publishers, 1996), p. 105.

10. Bruce McDowell and Anees Zaka, *Muslims and Christians at the Table* (Phillipsburg, NJ: Presbyterian and Reformed Publishing, 1999), p. 45.

11. Mather and Nichols, p. 141.

12. Goldmann, p. 18.

13. Based on Goldmann, p. 19.

14. Jamal Elias, *Islam* (Englewood Cliffs, NJ: Prentice Hall, 1999), p. 73.

15. Frederick Mathewson Denny, *An Introduction to Islam* (New York: Macmillan Publishers, 1985), p. 136.

16. Elias, p. 73.

17. John Ankerberg and John Weldon, *Fast Facts on Islam* (Eugene, OR: Harvest House Publishers, 2001), p. 105.

18. Ergun Mehmet Caner and Emir Fethi Caner, *Unveiling Islam: An Insider's Look at Muslim Life and Beliefs* (Grand Rapids: Kregel, 2002), p. 49.

19. Goldmann, p. 22.

20. Ankerberg and Weldon, p. 19.

21. Quoted in Caner and Caner, pp. 183-84.

22. McDowell and Zaka, p. 26.

23. William Miller, *A Christian's Response to Islam* (Phillipsburg, NJ: Presbyterian and Reformed Publishing, 1976), p. 102.

Chapter 2—The Quran: The Scripture of Islam

1. Winfried Corduan, *Islam: A Christian Introduction* (Downers Grove, IL: InterVarsity Press, 1998), p. 11.

2. Jamal Elias, *Islam* (Englewood Cliffs, NJ: Prentice Hall, 1999), p. 21.

3. Ibid., p. 21.

4. David Goldmann, *Islam and the Bible* (Chicago: Moody Publishers, 2004), p. 58.

5. Ibid., p. 70.

6. Geoffrey Parrinder, *World Religions* (New York: Facts on File Publications, 1971), p. 473.

7. Mishkat III, p. 664, in *The World of Islam* CD-ROM (Colorado Springs: Global Mapping International, 2000).

8. Elias, p. 21.

9. William M. Miller, *A Christian's Response to Islam* (Phillipsburg, NJ: Presbyterian and Reformed Publishing, 1976), p. 53. Bruce McDowell and Anees Zaka, *Muslims and Christians at the Table* (Phillipsburg, NJ: Presbyterian and Reformed Publishing, 1999), p. 72.

10. Badru Kateregga and David W. Shenk, *A Muslim and a Christian in Dialogue* (Scottdale, PA: Herald Press, 1997), n.p.

11. Lewis Hopfe, *Religions of the World* (New York: Macmillan Publishers, 1991), p. 408.

12. Harold Berry, *Islam: What They Believe* (Lincoln, NE: Back to the Bible Publishing, 1992), p. 18.

13. Ergun Mehmet Caner and Emir Fethi Caner, *Unveiling Islam* (Grand Rapids: Kregel, 2002), p. 86.

14. Elias, p. 20.

15. H.U. Stanton, *The Teaching of the Quran* (New York: Bible and Tannen, 1969), pp. 10-11.

16. Norman Geisler and Abdul Saleeb, *Answering Islam* (Grand Rapids: Baker Books, 1993), p. 91.

17. McDowell and Zaka, pp. 74-75.

18. Maului Muhammad Ali, *Muhammad and Christ* (Lahore, India: The Ahmadiyya Anjuman-i-Ishaat-i-Islam, 1921), p. 7.

19. Susanne Haneef, *What Everyone Should Know About Islam and Muslims* (Chicago: Kazi, 1979), pp. 18-19.

20. Kateregga and Shenk, *A Muslim and a Christian in Dialogue,* n.p.

21. Elias, p. 25.

22. Gerhard Nehls, *Christians Ask Muslims,* in *The World of Islam* CD-ROM (Colorado Springs: Global Mapping International, 2000).

23. Christi Wilson, *Introducing Islam* (New York: Friendship Press, 1958), p. 30.

24. Kateregga and Shenk, *A Muslim and a Christian in Dialogue,* n.p.

25. Goldmann, p. 23.

26. Alfred Guillaume, cited in Gerhard Nehls, *Christians Ask Muslims.*

27. Adrian Brockett, "The Value of the Hafs and Warsh Transmissions for the Textual History of the Quran," in *Approaches to the History of the Interpretation of the Quran,* ed. Andrew Rippin (Oxford: Clarendon Press, 1988), pp. 34, 37.

28. Geisler and Saleeb, p. 194.

29. Ibid., p. 187.

30. Ali Dashti, *Twenty Three Years* (London: Allen and Unwin, 1985), pp. 48, 50.

31. Nehls, *Christians Ask Muslims*, n.p.

32. Walter Martin, *The Kingdom of the Cults* (Bloomington, MN: Bethany House Publishers, 1999).

33. Gleason Archer, "Confronting the Challenge of Islam in the 21st Century," *Contend for the Faith* (Chicago: Evangelical Ministries to New Religions, 1992), p. 106.

34. Frederick Mathewson Denny, *An Introduction to Islam* (New York: Macmillan Publishers, 1994), p. 159.

Chapter 3—Muhammad: The Prophet of Islam

1. William Miller, *A Christian's Response to Islam* (Phillipsburg, NJ: Presbyterian and Reformed Publishing, 1976), p. 51.

2. Badru Kateregga and David Shenk, *A Muslim and a Christian in Dialogue* (Scottdale, PA: Herald Press, 1997), in *The World of Islam* CD-ROM (Colorado Springs: Global Mapping International, 2000).

3. John Noss, *Man's Religions* (New York: Macmillan Publishers, 1974), p. 518.

4. Norman Geisler and Abdul Saleeb, *Answering Islam* (Grand Rapids: Baker Books, 1993), p. 52.

5. Noss, p. 511.

6. Ibid., p. 509.

7. Gerald Berry, *Religions of the World* (Lincoln, NE: Back to the Bible Publishing, 1992), p. 60.

8. Berry, p. 80; Josh McDowell and Don Stewart, *Handbook of Today's Religions* (San Bernardino: Here's Life Publishers, 1989), p. 379.

9. Kenneth Boa, *Cults, World Religions, and You* (Wheaton: Victor Books, 1977), p. 49.

10. George Mather and Larry Nichols, *Dictionary of Cults, Sects, Religions and the Occult* (Grand Rapids: Zondervan, 1993), p. 139; Lewis Hopfe, *Religions of the World* (New York: Macmillan Publishers, 1991), p. 402.

11. David Bradley, *A Guide to the World's Religions* (Englewood Cliffs, NJ: Prentice Hall, 1963), p. 68.

12. Bruce McDowell and Anees Zaka, *Muslims and Christians at the Table* (Phillipsburg, NJ: Presbyterian and Reformed Publishing, 1999), p. 32.

13. Geoffrey Parrinder, *World Religions* (New York: Facts on File Publications, 1971), p. 466.

14. Hopfe, p. 403.

15. Miller, p. 20.

16. Hopfe, p. 404.

17. Samuel Zwemer, *The Muslim Christ* (New York: American Tract Society, 1912), in *The World of Islam* CD-ROM (Colordo Springs: Global Mapping International, 2000).

18. Dean Halverson, *The Compact Guide to World Religions* (Bloomington, MN: Bethany House Publishers, 1996), p. 104.

19. Reza Safa, *Inside Islam* (Lake Mary, FL: Charisma House, 1996), p. 27.

20. Boa, p. 51.

21. Miller, p. 28.

22. George Braswell, *What You Need to Know About Islam and Muslims* (Nashville: Broadman and Holman Publishing Group, 2000), p. 2.

23. Jamal Elias, *Islam* (Englewood Cliffs, NJ: Prentice Hall, 1999), p. 35.

24. McDowell and Zaka, p. 37.

25. William J. Saal, *Reaching Muslims for Christ* (Chicago: Moody Press, 1993), n.p.

26. Robert Morey, "Common Logical Fallacies Made by Muslims" (Research Education Foundation, 1996). Available online at 222.chick.com/internationalreligions/Islam/fallacies.asp.

27. McDowell and Zaka, p. 36.

28. John Ankerberg and John Weldon, *Fast Facts on Islam* (Eugene, OR: Harvest House Publishers, 2001), p. 10.

Chapter 4—Allah: The God of Islam

1. William Miller, *A Christian's Response to Islam* (Phillipsburg, NJ: Presbyterian and Reformed Publishing, 1976), p. 45.

2. Bruce McDowell and Anees Zaka, *Muslims and Christians at the Table* (Phillipsburg, NJ: Presbyterian and Reformed Publishing, 1999), p. 94.

3. Donald Tingle, *Islam and Christianity* (Downers Grove, IL: InterVarsity Press, 1985), p. 8.

4. Abdiyah Akbar Abdul-Haqq, *Sharing Your Faith with a Muslim* (Bloomington, MN: Bethany House Publishers, 1980), p. 159.

5. Risaleh-i-Barkhawi, quoted in Gerhard Nehls, *Christians Ask Muslims,* in *The World of Islam* CD-ROM (Colorado Springs: Global Mapping International, 2000).

6. Lewis Hopfe, *Religions of the World* (New York: Macmillan Publishers, 1991), p. 410.

7. McDowell and Zaka, p. 124.

8. Norman Geisler and Abdul Saleeb, *Answering Islam* (Grand Rapids: Baker Books, 1993), pp. 141-42.

9. Ergun Mehmet Caner and Emir Fethi Caner, *Unveiling Islam* (Grand Rapids: Kregel, 2002), p. 117.

10. Sobhi Malek, *Islam: Challenge and Mandate,* in *The World of Islam* CD-ROM (Colorado Springs: Global Mapping International, 2000).

11. William Saal, *Reaching Muslims for Christ* (Chicago: Moody Publishers, 1993), n.p.

12. Dean Halverson, *The Compact Guide to World Religions* (Bloomington, MN: Bethany House Publishers, 1996), p. 113.

13. Gleason Archer, "Confronting the Challenge of Islam in the 21st Century," *Contend for the Faith* (Chicago: Evangelical Ministries to New Religions, 1992), p. 99.

Chapter 5—Muslims' Five Primary Duties

1. The Institute for the Study of Islam and Christianity, *Survey of Islam,* Section Six: "Islam—The Practice," in *The World of Islam* CD-ROM (Colorado Springs: Global Mapping International, 2000).

2. Jamal Elias, *Islam* (Englewood Cliffs, NJ: Prentice Hall, 1999), p. 66.

3. Ibid.

4. See Everett Hullum, *Beliefs of Other Kinds* (Atlanta: Baptist Home Mission Board, 1984), p. 121.

5. David Goldmann, *Islam and the Bible* (Chicago: Moody Publishers, 2004), p. 114.

6. George Braswell, *What You Need to Know About Islam and Muslims* (Nashville: Broadman and Holman Publishers, 2000), p. 33.

7. Lewis Hopfe, *Religions of the World* (New York: Macmillan Publishers, 1991), p. 415.

8. Winfried Corduan, *Islam* (Downers Grove, IL: InterVarsity Press, 1998), p. 17.

9. Dean Halverson, *The Compact Guide to World Religions* (Bloomington, MN: Bethany House Publishers, 1996), p. 107.

10. Ergun Mehmet Caner and Emir Fethi Caner, *Unveiling Islam* (Grand Rapids: Kregel, 2002), pp. 123-24.

11. Ibid., p. 124.

12. Frederick Mathewson Denny, *An Introduction to Islam* (New York: Macmillan Publishers, 1985), p. 120.

13. Braswell, p. 34.

14. Goldmann, p. 118.

15. Caner and Caner, p. 125.

16. Hopfe, p. 416.

17. William Miller, *A Christian's Response to Islam* (Phillipsburg, NJ: Presbyterian and Reformed Publishing, 1976), p. 59.

18. Bruce McDowell and Anees Zaka, *Muslims and Christians at the Table* (Phillipsburg, NJ: Presbyterian and Reformed Publishing, 1999), p. 60.

19. George Mather and Larry Nichols, *Dictionary of Cults, Sects, Religions and the Occult* (Grand Rapids: Zondervan, 1993), p. 142.

20. Miller, p. 59.

21. Denny, p. 126.

22. Ravi Zacharias, *Jesus Among Other Gods* (Nashville: W Publishing Group, 2000), p. 98.

23. Mather and Nichols, p. 142.

24. Caner and Caner, p. 130.

25. Abdulkader Tayob, *Islam: A Short Introduction* (Oxford: Oneworld Publications, 1999), p. 99.

26. Denny, p. 132.

27. Ibid.

28. John Noss, *Man's Religions* (New York: Macmillan Publishers, 1974), p. 524.

29. Ibid., p. 510.

30. Halverson, p. 107.

31. McDowell and Zaka, p. 58.

32. Elias, p. 73.

33. Braswell, p. 2.

Chapter 6—Allah and Salvation

1. Badru Kateregga and David Shenk, *A Muslim and a Christian in Dialogue* (Scottdale, PA: Herald Press, 1997), p. 18.

2. J. Dudley Woodberry, *Dimensions of Witness Among Muslims* (Seoul, Korea: Chongshin University, 1997), in *The World of Islam* CD-ROM (Colorado Springs: Global Mapping International, 2000).

3. Isma'il Al Faruqi, *Islam* (Niles, IL: Arugus Communications, 1984), p. 9.

4. Ergun Mehmet Caner and Emir Fethi Caner, *Unveiling Islam* (Grand Rapids: Kregel, 2002), p. 18.

5. Ibid., pp. 31-32.

6. Ibid., p. 32.

7. John Ankerberg and John Weldon, *Encyclopedia of Cults and New Religions* (Eugene, OR: Harvest House Publishers, 1999), p. 517.

8. William Saal, *Reaching Muslims for Christ* (Chicago: Moody Publishers, 1993), n.p.

Chapter 7—Judgment Day, Heaven, and Hell

1. William Miller, *A Christian's Response to Islam* (Phillipsburg, NJ: Presbyterian and Reformed Publishing, 1976), p. 56.

2. Ibid., p. 82.

3. Quoted in Harold J. Berry, *Islam* (Lincoln, NE: Back to the Bible Publishing, 1992), p. 42.

4. Ergun Mehmet Caner and Emir Fethi Caner, *Unveiling Islam* (Grand Rapids: Kregel, 2002), p. 149.

5. Phil Parshall, *The Cross and the Crescent* (Wheaton: Tyndale House Publishers, 1989), n.p.

6. Ibid.

7. Lewis Hopfe, *Religions of the World* (New York: Macmillan Publishers, 1991), p. 412.

8. George Braswell, *What You Need to Know About Islam and Muslims* (Nashville: Broadman and Holman Publishers, 2000), p. 30.

9. Gerald Berry, *Religions of the World* (New York: Barnes & Noble, 1956), p. 64.

10. Miller, p. 56.

11. Jamal Elias, *Islam* (Englewood Cliffs, NJ: Prentice Hall, 1999), p. 65.

12. Phil Parshall, *Inside the Community* (Grand Rapids: Baker Books, 1994), n.p.

13. Ibid.

14. John Elder, *The Biblical Approach to the Muslim* (Madison, GA: Source of Light Ministries International, 2000), n.p.

15. Ibid.

Chapter 8—Has the Bible Been Corrupted?

1. Gleason Archer, "Confronting the Challenge of Islam in the 21st Century," *Contend for the Faith* (Chicago: Evangelical Ministries to New Religions, 1992), p. 97.

2. Alhaj Ajijola, *The Essence of Faith in Islam* (Lahore, Pakistan: Islamic Publications, 1978), p. 79.

3. Gerhard Nehls, *Christians Answer Muslims,* in *The World of Islam* CD-ROM (Colorado Springs: Global Imaging International, 2000).

4. Maurice Bucaille, *The Bible, The Quran, and Science* (Lahore, Pakistan: Darulfikr, 1977), p. 9.

5. Larry A. Poston with Carl F. Ellis, Jr., *The Changing Face of Islam in America* (Camp Hill, PA: Horizon Books Publishers, 2000), p. 183.

6. Martin Goldsmith, *Islam and Christian Witness* (Carlisle, Cumbria, England: OM Publishing, 1998).

7. John Gilchrist, "The Textual History of the Qur'an and the Bible" (Rikon, Switzerland: The Good Way). Available online at www.the-good-way. com/eng/article/a02.htm.

8. Bucaille, p. vi.

9. Quoted in Nehls, *Christians Answer Muslims.*

10. Ahmed Deedat, *Is the Bible God's Word?* (Durban, South Africa: Islamic Propagation Centre International), p. 2.

11. W. St. Clair Tisdall, *Christian Reply to Muslim Objections* (London: Society for Promoting Christian Knowledge, 1904).

12. William Saal, *Reaching Muslims for Christ* (Chicago: Moody Publishers, 1993), n.p.

13. Norman Geisler and Abdul Saleeb, *Answering Islam* (Grand Rapids: Baker Books, 1993), p. 212.

14. Greg Bahnsen, "The Inerrancy of the Autographa," in *Inerrancy*, ed. Norman Geisler (Grand Rapids: Zondervan, 1980), p. 161.

15. See B.M. Metzger, *The Text of the New Testament*, 3rd ed. (New York: Oxford University Press USA, 1992); B.M. Metzger, *The Early Versions of the New Testament* (Oxford: Clarendon Press, 1977); B.D. Ehrman and M.W. Holmes, eds., *The Text of the New Testament in Contemporary Research* (Grand Rapids: Eerdmans Publishing Company, 1995).

16. Norman Geisler and William Nix, *A General Introduction to the Bible* (Chicago: Moody Publishers, 1978), p. 357.

17. Winfried Corduan, *Islam* (Downers Grove, IL: InterVarsity Press, 1998), p. 29.

18. Gleason Archer, *A Survey of Old Testament Introduction* (Chicago: Moody Publishers, 1964), p. 19.

19. Ibid., p. 98.

20. Quoted in Gilchrist, "The Textual History of the Qur'an and the Bible."

21. Bucaille, p. vi.

Chapter 9—Was Jesus Merely a Prophet?

1. Bruce McDowell and Anees Zaka, *Muslims and Christians at the Table* (Phillipsburg, NJ: Presbyterian and Reformed Publishing, 1999), p. 108.

2. Cited in David Goldmann, *Islam and the Bible* (Chicago: Moody Publishers, 2004), p. 36.

3. William Miller, *A Christian's Response to Islam* (Phillipsburg, NJ: Presbyterian and Reformed Publishing, 1976), p. 77.

4. Ahmed Deedat, *Christ in Islam* (Durban, South Africa: Islamic Propagation Center). Available online at www.jamaat.net/cis/ChristianIslam.html.

5. W. St. Clair Tisdall, *Christian Reply to Muslim Objections* (London: Society for Promoting Christian Knowledge, 1904).

6. Deedat, *Christ in Islam.*

7. Larry A. Poston with Carl F. Ellis, Jr., *The Changing Face of Islam in America* (Camp Hill, PA: Horizon Books Publishers, 2000), p. 188.

8. Abdiyah Akbar Abdul-Haqq, *Sharing Your Faith with a Muslim* (Bloomington, MN: Bethany House Publishers, 1980), n.p.

9. Debate between Josh McDowell and Ahmed Deedat, August 1981, Durban, South Africa. Transcript available online at www.ais.org/~maftab/debate.html.

10. Ahmed Deedat, *Resurrection or Resuscitation?* Available online at www.ais.org/~maftab/resurc.

11. See John Gilchrist, "The Textual History of the Qur'an and the Bible" (Rikon, Switzerland: The Good Way). Available online at www.the-good-way.com/eng/article/a02.htm.

12. Dean Halverson, *The Compact Guide to World Religions* (Bloomington, MN: Bethany House Publishers, 1996), p. 114.

13. John Haines, *Good News for Muslims* (Philadelphia: Middle East Resources, 1998), p. 66.

14. Norman Geisler and Abdul Saleeb, *Answering Islam* (Grand Rapids: Baker Books, 1993), p. 227.

15. Harold J. Berry, *Islam: What They Believe* (Lincoln, NE: Back to the Bible Publishing, 1992), p. 33.

Chapter 10—Dialoguing with Muslims

1. Max Kershaw, *How to Share the Good News With Your Muslim Friend* (Colorado Springs: International Students Inc., 2000), p. 3.

2. Phil Parshall, *The Fortress and the Fire* (Worli, India: Gospel Literature Service, 1975), p. 104.

3. John Gilchrist, *The Christian Witness to the Muslim*, in *The World of Islam* CD-ROM (Colorado Springs: Global Mapping International, 2000).

4. William Miller, *A Christian's Response to Islam* (Phillipsburg, NJ: Presbyterian and Reformed Publishing, 1976), p. 134.

5. Dean Halverson, *The Compact Guide to World Religions* (Bloomington, MN: Bethany House Publishers, 1996), p. 109.

6. Bruce McDowell and Anees Zaka, *Muslims and Christians at the Table* (Phillipsburg, NJ: Presbyterian and Reformed Publishing, 1999), pp. 62-63.

7. Sobhi Malek, *Islam: Challenge and Mandate*, in *The World of Islam* CD-ROM (Colorado Springs: Global Mapping International, 2000).

8. Ibid.

9. Donald Tingle, *Islam & Christianity* (Downers Grove, IL: InterVarsity Press, 1985), p. 3.

10. Larry A. Poston with Carl F. Ellis, Jr., *The Changing Face of Islam in America* (Camp Hill, PA: Horizon Books Publishers, 2000), p. 238.

11. See David Goldmann, *Islam and the Bible* (Chicago: Moody Press, 2004), p. 144.

12. David Reed, *Jehovah's Witnesses: Answered Verse by Verse* (Grand Rapids: Baker Books, 1992), p. 115.

13. Ergun Mehmet Caner and Emir Fethi Caner, *Unveiling Islam* (Grand Rapids: Kregel, 2002), p. 225.

14. William Saal, *Reaching Muslims for Christ* (Chicago: Moody Press, 1993), n.p.

15. Ibid.

16. Reza Safa, *Inside Islam* (Lake Mary, FL: Charisma House, 1996), p. 94.

17. Halverson, p. 109.

BIBLIOGRAPHY

Anderson, Sir Norman. *Islam in the Modern World.* Leicester, England: InterVarsity Press, 1990.

Ankerberg, John, and John Weldon. *Fast Facts on Islam.* Eugene, OR: Harvest House, 2001.

Berry, Harold J. *Islam: What They Believe.* Lincoln, NE: Back to the Bible Publishing, 1992.

Braswell, George. *What You Need to Know About Islam and Muslims.* Nashville: Broadman and Holman Publishers, 2000.

Bucaille, Maurice. *The Bible, the Quran, and Science.* Pakistan: Durulfikr, 1977.

Caner, Ergun Mehmet and Emir Fethi Caner. *Unveiling Islam.* Grand Rapids: Kregel, 2002.

Chapman, Colin. *Cross and Crescent: Responding to the Challenge of Islam.* Downers Grove, IL: InterVarsity Press, 2003.

———. *Going Soft on Islam? Reflections on Some Evangelical Responses to Islam.* London: London Bible College, 1989.

Cooper, Anne, compiler. *Ishmael My Brother: A Biblical Course on Islam.* Tunbridge Wells, England: Evangelical Missionary Alliance, 1993.

Corduan, Winfried. *Islam: A Christian Introduction.* Downers Grove, IL: InterVarsity Press, 1998.

Denny, Frederick Mathewson. *An Introduction to Islam.* New York: Macmillan Publishers, 1994.

Elder, John. *The Biblical Approach to the Muslim.* Madison, GA: Source of Light Ministries International, 2000.

Elias, Jamal J. *Islam.* Englewood Cliffs, NJ: Prentice Hall, 1999.

Geisler, Norman, and Abdul Saleeb. *Answering Islam: The Crescent in the Light of the Cross.* Grand Rapids: Baker Books, 1993.

Goldmann, David. *Islam and the Bible: Why Two Faiths Collide.* Chicago: Moody Press, 2004.

Goldsmith, Martin, *Islam and Christian Witness.* Carlisle, Cumbria, England: OM Publishing, 1998.

Haines, John. *Good News for Muslims.* Philadelphia: Middle East Resources, 1998.

Jones, Bevan. *Christianity Explained to Muslims: A Manual for Christian Workers.* Calcutta: YMCA Publishing House, 1938.

Kateregga, Badru D., and David W. Shenk. *A Muslim and a Christian in Dialogue.* Scottdale, PA: Herald Press, 1997.

Kershaw, R. Max. *How to Share the Good News with Your Muslim Friend.* Colorado Springs: International Students Inc., 2000.

McDowell, Bruce A., and Anees Zaka. *Muslims and Christians at the Table.* Phillipsburg, NJ: Presbyterian and Reformed Publishing, 1999.

Miller, William M. *A Christian's Response to Islam.* Phillipsburg, NJ: Presbyterian and Reformed Publishing, 1976.

Morey, Robert. *The Islamic Invasion.* Eugene, OR: Harvest House Publishers, 1992.

Parshall, Phil. *Inside the Community: Understanding Muslims Through Their Traditions.* Grand Rapids: Baker Books, 1994.

———. *The Cross and the Crescent: Understanding the Muslim Mind and Heart.* Wheaton, IL: Tyndale House Publishers, 1989.

Poston, Larry A., and Carl F. Ellis. *The Changing Face of Islam in America.* Camp Hill, PA: Horizon Books Publishers, 2000.

Rhodes, Ron. *Islam: What You Need to Know.* Eugene, OR: Harvest House Publishers, 2000.

Saal, William J. *Reaching Muslims for Christ.* Chicago: Moody Press, 1993.

Safa, Reza F. *Inside Islam.* Lake Mary, FL: Charisma House, 1996.

Tayob, Abdulkader. *Islam: A Short Introduction*. Oxford, England: Oneworld Publications, 1999.

Tisdall, W. St. Clair. *Christian Reply to Muslim Objections*. London: Society for Promoting Christian Knowledge, 1904.

Watt, W. Montgomery, and Richard Bell. *Bell's Introduction to the Quran*. Edinburgh: Edinburgh University Press, 1970.

Woodberry, J. Dudley. *Dimensions of Witness Among Muslims*. Seoul, Korea: Chongshin University, 1997.

Zwemer, Samuel M. *The Muslim Christ*. New York: American Tract Society, 1912.

CROSSINGS®
THE BOOK CLUB FOR TODAY'S CHRISTIAN FAMILY

A Letter to Our Readers

Dear Reader:

In order that we might better contribute to your reading enjoyment, we would appreciate your taking a few minutes to respond to the following questions. When completed, please return to the following:

Andrea Doering, Editor-in-Chief
Crossings Book Club
401 Franklin Avenue, Garden City, NY 11530

You can post your review online! Go to www.crossings.com and rate this book.

Title _____ Author _____

1 Did you enjoy reading this book?

❑ Very much. I would like to see more books by this author!

❑ I really liked_____

❑ Moderately. I would have enjoyed it more if_____

2 What influenced your decision to purchase this book? Check all that apply.

    ❑ Cover
    ❑ Title
    ❑ Publicity
    ❑ Catalog description
    ❑ Friends
    ❑ Enjoyed other books by this author
    ❑ Other _____

3 Please check your age range:

    ❑ Under 18   ❑ 18-24
    ❑ 25-34   ❑ 35-45
    ❑ 46-55   ❑ Over 55

4 How many hours per week do you read? _____

5 How would you rate this book, on a scale from 1 (poor) to 5 (superior)?
_____

Name_____

Occupation_____

Address_____

City_____ State_____ Zip_____